HOW TO RISK-PROOF YOUR KIDS

HOW TO RISK-PROOF YOUR KIDS

Kathleen Winkler

To Ralph, my partner in parenting,
and to Brad and Kristin, who made it joy-filled.

All scripture quotations are taken from the HOLY BIBLE, NEW INTERNATIONAL VERSION®. NIV®. Copyright © 1973, 1978, 1984 by International Bible Society. Used by permission of Zondervan Publishing House. All rights reserved.

Copyright © 1996 Concordia Publishing House
3558 S. Jefferson Avenue, St. Louis, MO 63118-3968
Manufactured in the United States of America

All rights reserved. No part of this publication may be reproduced, stored in a retrieval system, or transmitted, in any form or by any means, electronic, mechanical, photocopying, recording, or otherwise, without the prior written permission of Concordia Publishing House.

1 2 3 4 5 6 7 8 9 10   05 04 03 02 01 00 99 98 97 96

Contents

As You Begin — 7

1. Pass on Your Values to Your Kids — 9
2. Turn Off the Media's Corrupting Influence — 22
3. Mute Rock's Raucous Message — 31
4. Encourage Cross-cultural Education — 46
5. Uncover the Problems of Promiscuity — 56
6. Expose Abortion's Big Lie — 69
7. Deflate the High of Alcohol and Drugs — 79
8. Deglamorize Gangs, Guns, and Violence — 94
9. Guard Against Depression and Suicide — 107
10. Fight Eating Disorders — 120
11. Arm Your Kids to Battle Satanism — 132

As You Begin

13-year-old Shot Girl, [age] 12, Police Say
(Town) Tries to Deter Teen Drinking
Boy Hoped to Sell LSD at Mall, Police Say

Those headlines came from last night's newspaper in my city. During the previous weeks there have been other headlines: about the rising number of children born to single teen mothers, about the escalating rates of sexually transmitted diseases among teens, about the latest rock star to be arrested for drug possession or violence.

Temptations are everywhere our kids are. Destructive conduct is glamorized. Walking the moral path is mocked. Values are under assault on every side.

It's a dangerous world our children are walking into. The temptations they face too often carry the risk of tragedy and death. They hear, as if from a battery of speakers surrounding them, a constant drumbeat: Do it! Have fun! Don't worry about the future! Go for the pleasure today!

Even if sheltered within the loving walls of a Christian home, kids have to grow up, head out, and face the temptations the world places before them.

It's a tough time to be a teen. It's also a tough time to be a parent. Let's face it, you can't keep your kids tucked behind the walls of your home forever. You can't shield them. They have to face the world—along with all the glitter, glamour, and temptation it holds.

What's a parent to do?

The only thing you can do is try to prepare your

children for what they are going to face. Build within them a solid core of values they can cling to. Educate them about the dangers temptations hold. So equipped, your children will have the best chance of withstanding the onslaught.

My own kids have safely arrived at young adulthood. The journey they made through adolescence was fraught with the same dangers your kids will face. I thank God every day that they made it. I don't claim to be any expert at parenting—it was God's grace that surrounded my kids.

But there are people out there who are experts: doctors, psychologists, educators, and ministers. And they have a wealth of information to share about making the journey through adolescence safer for your kids. I've sought them out, collected their wisdom, added the wisdom of some parents in the trenches and a few thoughts of my own, and come up with some practical helps for parents whose kids are beginning to navigate the waters of adolescence.

Most of the experts allowed me to use their real names. I've indicated the few who didn't. The names of all the teens and parents have been changed to protect their privacy.

I hope their ideas will help you. Learn what you can from them, then trust that God's hand will stretch over your child during the teen years. God gave the gift of His Son as a sacrifice to earn forgiveness and new life for you and your child. He will not let you down.

Kathy Winkler

1

Pass on Your Values to Your Kids

And What to Do When the World's Values Conflict

"Let's have some fun. You know those bottle rockets we made? If you put them in mailboxes and set them off, kaboom! The whole mailbox goes up! Wanna do that tonight?"

"Hey, let's go over to Jason's after the eighth-grade dance Friday night. He said he could get us some beer from his father's stuff in the basement. There's so much down there his dad'll never miss it!"

"Aw, come on, Shelley. All the girls give a lot more than you do. Don't you love me? If you did, we'd do a little more."

Children, preteens, and teenagers face temptations at every turn. James Dobson, in his book *Children at Risk*, describes the teen years as a passage down a long hallway lined with doors. Behind those doors are drugs, alcohol, sexual promiscuity, and a host of other temptations. When most present-day parents were growing up, those doors were open only a crack. We all knew some kids who drank or had sex, but they were in the minority.

Today those doors are not only wide open, Dobson says, they've been taken off their hinges! "Never in history has a culture discarded its belief system more quickly than America did in the sixties," he writes. "Historic perspectives on morality and ethics gave way to a 'new morality' based on changing social attitudes. Prohibitions dissolved, rules changed, restrictions faded, and guilt subsided."[1]

We are paying the price for that rejection of values. Look at the enormous increase in divorce, the high percentages of those suffering from alcoholism and drug addiction, the explosion of teen pregnancies, and the frightening epidemic of sexually transmitted diseases. It's more important than ever that our kids have a foundation of values to help them traverse the long corridor to adulthood.

As parents, we can preach for endless hours about the dangers behind the doors, but ultimately our kids will choose for themselves whether to open the doors and walk inside. We can't be there to shut the doors. All we can do is give them the Christ-centered foundation that will enable them to say, "No, thanks. I don't want to do that. Count me out."

But how do you give kids those kinds of values? I don't think our parents needed to sit down with us and talk specifically about values. The whole community modeled them. They may not have been labeled "Christian" values, but they were solid. Values were reinforced in the schools, and they weren't torn down in the media. Kids sort of absorbed them by osmosis.

It's different today. The schools have become "value free." The entertainment world actively promotes harmful values. The temptations are much stronger and more open. You can't assume, as our parents did, that modeling values is enough. You have to teach them in a systematic way—in the home.

A System for Teaching Values

Perry Bresemann, principal of a Lutheran elementary school in Elm Grove, Wisconsin, and his faculty have developed a systematic approach to teaching values that I wish I'd had when my kids were growing up. It's based on the simple phrase, "Just a little RESPECT."

"First, values have to be defined," Bresemann says. "In order to say we are going to teach Christian values to our children, we have to define what Christian values are."

Teaching values is really teaching children to take what they have learned from Scripture and put it into action in daily life. "Values are the bridge, if you will, between Scripture and decision-making," Bresemann says.

The school faculty spent long hours one summer asking exactly what they wanted the children to do, based on Christian principles. "We listed everything we could think of, and we found they all boiled down to six statements built around the concept of respect," Bresemann explains.

The RESPECT program is now in place at every level in the school. It also has been shared, via a personal visit, with every parent. The RESPECT poster hangs in each classroom and decorates the refrigerator door in many homes. "More parents than I can count have told me how helpful this program is," Bresemann says. "When they see a misbehavior, they can say, 'You aren't showing respect for ...' We've given them a tool for home discipline."

There's nothing complicated about the six RESPECT statements. Their power lies in their simplicity. They provide a framework from which to hang values. But judge for yourself—here are the six statements.

As a member of this family, I will show respect for:

- **God and His Word.** "This is the number one value children need to have," Bresemann says. "If children are taught to respect God, they will already have the core they need." We can do nothing but wholeheartedly agree with this statement. In His Word, God gives us the Good News of the salvation His Son won for us on the cross. It is this great sacrifice that won forgiveness for the times we fail to live out Jesus' love and the times we fail to model that love for our children. God claims you and your children in Baptism. Regular worship and partaking of the Lord's Supper are valuable resources as the Holy Spirit helps you live out your respect for God and His Word.

- **Those in Authority.** This value starts in the home as parents teach their children to respect them. Then the value is broadened to include others in authority—teachers, obviously, but law enforcement officials, playground supervisors, and many others. "The value for respecting all people starts with people in authority," Bresemann says.

- **Our Classmates and Other People.** "Here we've

said not only do you need to respect those in authority, but you also need to respect your peers," Bresemann says. "Each person is valuable. Christ died for each one and gave them value and worth, therefore, we owe them respect." Then the circle is broadened to include friends and neighbors, and eventually children learn that respect applies to everyone in the world.

- **Our Bodies and Our God-Given Talents.** "Now we talk about ourselves," Bresemann continues. "We tell kids, 'You are special, created by God and saved by His Son to be respected and valued.' " Some people worry that teaching this concept will make kids self-centered, but when properly taught, it doesn't. It creates a child who feels good about herself and sees a reason to value someone else. "You can't show respect for someone else until you first respect yourself," Bresemann explains.

- **The Learning Process and the Classroom Environment.** While this statement seems to apply only to school, it actually has ramifications for the home also. Valuing education starts when children are very young. If parents respect education and share that with their children, the children will come to school feeling it's an important place, one in which they want to do well.

- **Our School and Personal Property and the Property of Others.** Again written for the school, this value extends into the home—as well as the park, the grocery store, and anywhere else a child goes.

"If you look at the whole system, you can see that it creates a framework, a core for us to teach values," Bresemann says.

How do you implement the RESPECT program in your home? It's most effective if begun while your children are young, but even if your kids are already in the middle grades, it's not too late. Bresemann offers some suggestions:

- **Put the concept of respect into terminology your children can understand.** You might start with the word *trust* by saying, "You want me to trust you, to believe what you say. That means you want me to put value in what you say, to respect it." From there you can build the concept of respect.

- **Model respect to your children.** You can't demand respect and not give it in return. One thing the Elm Grove faculty did that parents can do also was to take a long, hard look at the discipline techniques they were using. If a technique wasn't acceptable under the RESPECT guidelines, it wasn't used.

- **Agree with your spouse to monitor each other's discipline techniques.** Give each other permission to say (privately, of course, not in front of your child), "What you did wasn't modeling respect" until a more respectful pattern becomes second nature. Together, parents and children should ask God's forgiveness and forgive one another when respect isn't modeled.

- **For older children who understand the concept of respect, sit down and talk about the six statements.** Draw up a contract that states both you and your child will try to use the RESPECT model as your basis for relationships from now on. Post it in a prominent place where everyone can see it and be reminded of the agreement.

"Any parent who is trying to teach values in a valueless environment has a very hard job," Bresemann says. "But if you can get a child to understand the concept of respect in a framework that places respect for God on top, it's going to serve you both well down the road."

When Values Conflict

It would be wonderful if the values you are instilling in your child at home were supported everywhere else in your community. That's the African concept of "It takes a whole village to raise a child." But as we all know too well, it isn't happening in contemporary America. Sadly, in many instances, the institution we trust our children to for six hours a day—the school—doesn't reinforce Christian values either. In fact, it can be instilling the opposite of Christian values.

Jim and Marie ran into that situation more than once with their four children. Located 30 miles from the closest parochial school in an area with an academically high-quality public school system, they chose the public school option. "Academically, our children were well-served," Jim says. "But sometimes it was kind of scary, depending on the values of the teachers who were engaging the kids in dialog."

Their biggest concern was the curriculum's pervasive viewpoint that there are no absolute standards of right and wrong. The curriculum supported the idea that moral judgments are up to the individual—what's right for you may not be right for someone else. As Christians, we can't accept that viewpoint. There are indeed absolutes—God makes that very clear.

"It mainly showed up in the human growth and development curriculum," Marie says. "Those classes included a lot of values clarification and what they called decision-making. They would set up situations and the kids would talk about how they would deal with them. There were no absolutes. No right or wrong."

"You can base your values on the Ten Commandments, where stealing, for example, is always wrong," Jim says, "or you can set up a situation in which the kids might come to the conclusion that it isn't. I remember a conversation I had with one of the kids who said his class had decided that it was okay for [a] person to steal because he was poor. That's frightening."

"In the eighth grade they showed the kids contraceptive devices," Marie says. "I thought they were sending the message, 'Just in case you choose.' That gets back to what's right for you might not be right for someone else."

Jim and Marie did a lot of homework. Marie served on material-review committees. They read the textbooks and the study guides. And they went to the school. "I can't tell you how many times I said to them, 'I'm the parent. Don't do my job!'" Marie says. "Their answer was that too many parents aren't doing it." Sad, but probably true.

"Actually," Marie says, "we never asked the school

to change any programs. We just asked for an option for our kids." Their wish was granted. The school offered an alternate health class that was fact based and didn't go into sexual mores or values. That's one possible solution, if the school is willing.

Sally Anderson (not her real name) is a Christian and the principal of a public middle school. She's dealt with similar conflicts but from the other side of the desk.

Her biggest conflict with a parent was not over the sex education program but over the biology class that taught only the evolutionary viewpoint.

"You are always going to have conflicts because in the public sector you are dealing with a broad variety of viewpoints," Anderson points out. "What I try to do is create a climate of reasonable accommodation. You do that in two ways: by creating a climate of openness and by not allowing the emotional climate to become so charged that people can't sort through how they want the school to handle a particular issue."

To handle the conflict over the evolution issue, Anderson invited the parent, student, and the biology teacher to a meeting. "I helped the parent and student to see that, while they were not comfortable with the perspective being taught, it was the one required in the school's curriculum. They wanted the class taught from a creation approach. I explained that if that was the viewpoint they wanted, they would have to look for it in a parochial school. There are people in our community who do not share their faith, who would not want that viewpoint taught."

But, Anderson pointed out, there was no reason why the student couldn't share his view with the class.

"A student has the right to put his or her viewpoint into the public forum," she says. "It's not an unlimited right—kids can't proselytize in the classroom. But if there's a perspective they can bring from their religious beliefs to something they're studying, we want to create a forum where they can express that, where they feel entitled and valued."

Anderson offered the student a chance to speak to the class on his differing viewpoint or to allow him to invite a guest speaker to address the class on creationism. The family made the arrangements.

"There's no need to run into a brick wall," Anderson says. "You can find common ground if you take the time. But the school has to stay within the law. The First Amendment says government can't make any laws that would establish a religion, but it also says government can't make any that prohibit the free exercise of religion. Schools have to walk a tightrope between those parameters."

What should a Christian parent do when values conflicts arise? Here's a list of suggestions from Jim and Marie, Perry Bresemann, and Sally Anderson.

- **Prepare your children.** "We had regular family devotions, plus wide-ranging table talks that were a mix of Christian doctrine, politics, and social issues," Jim says. As a result their kids were well-aware of the debates about values going on in our society and knew how to defend their positions.

- **Be aware of what is being taught.** Besides reading their children's textbooks and study guides, Jim and Marie visited classes at every level, got to know the teachers, and attended school board meetings and open curriculum meetings. You do have the legal right to know what the school is teaching and to review the materials.

- **Get to know other parents.** You can work together to accomplish your goals.
- **Don't be afraid to stand up to your children for what you believe.** Sometimes kids object, saying their parents are making them look like "geeks." That's the hardest part, Marie says. But she told her kids, "I have to do this because I'm committed to what I believe." Standing up for what you believe according to God's Word will help your children do the same.
- **Don't be afraid to stand up to the school or to other parents.** Marie knows she and Jim were called "right-wingers" and other unflattering names behind their backs. "If I were told that to my face, I would again simply state that I'm committed to what I believe," she says.
- **Be realistic.** Don't expect a public school to teach specific Christian beliefs. That's not the school's job. And it's against the law. "Realize that if you choose a public school, you will be making a trade-off," says Anderson.
- **Be reasonable in what you request.** Demands for a complete change in programming may not be realistic. Asking the school for another option for your children may be.
- **Pick your battles.** "Decide if this is a hill you are willing to die on," says Bresemann. "If it's some-

thing you can counter by providing alternate instruction, then handle it that way." He suggests a preinstruction talk (this is what you are going to hear) followed by a postinstruction discussion. If the conflict is so severe that you are still uncomfortable, then you need to approach the school. Taking your child out of a class should be the last resort.

- **The way you approach the school will have a huge effect on what you accomplish.** "Do it in the spirit of finding common ground," says Anderson. "You want to keep your reaction as low on the emotional scale as you can. The lower your reaction, the more options you give the other person. Sometimes people immediately want to go to seven or eight emotionally, and that forces me to go to seven or eight too. If you stay at two or three, there are many more solutions."

- **Treat others with the same respect you wish to be accorded.** "Even if you are not treated respectfully, you must continue to be respectful," says Jim. "If people see you treating others with respect, that will make your views carry a great deal more weight." We model our Christian faith in the way we handle conflict as in all other things.

- **Model the importance of worship and turning to God's Word for your children.** Celebrate your children's baptism birthdays. Your children are not alone in their struggle to uphold Christian values. In their baptism, they are joined to Christ. They walk with Him, safely cradled in His arms.

The corridor lined with doors is there for your child as he or she moves into the world of adolescence. What's behind those doors can cause lifelong consequences. You can't always be with your kids, but you can give them a solid foundation of values to help them evaluate what's beckoning to them.

Centering our children in Jesus Christ is our primary duty as parents. And remember, we have the ultimate help on our side. The task would be impossible without God!

Further Reading

Brusius, Ron, ed. *Parenting Moral Teens in Immoral Times.* St. Louis: Concordia Publishing House, 1989.

Dobson, James C., and Gary L. Bauer. *Children at Risk: The Battle for the Hearts and Minds of Our Children.* Dallas: Word Inc., 1990.

Reed, Bobbie. *How to Have a Healthy Family: Even in Stressful Times.* St. Louis: Concordia Publishing House, 1995.

Notes

1. James C. Dobson and Gary L. Bauer, *Children at Risk: The Battle for the Hearts and Minds of Our Children,* (Dallas: Word Inc., 1990), p. 24.

2

Turn Off the Media's Corrupting Influence

"Cool it, Dad, don't have a cow!" the obnoxious Bart Simpson snaps at his long-suffering father who has had the temerity to correct Bart for something. What would have happened if you had spoken like this to your father? I would never have dared to say such a thing or use that tone of voice to mine.

Has your child ever spoken to you in that tone or said something similar? Christian parents increasingly need to cope with children who imitate the child/parent relationships they see on TV. One mother I know told her precocious 6-year-old in no uncertain terms, "I don't care if that's how families on TV talk to each other, we don't talk that way in our house. Ever."

Kids imitate what they see. That comes as no surprise to parents. The role model for families on television and in the movies used to be the much-maligned family of Ozzie and Harriet, in which the parents loved each other and their children, taught them values, offered guidance. Judging by the dismissive tone used in the media, such families are simply not with it in today's world. They have been replaced by a parade of dysfunctional TV and movie families in which boorish parents are regularly put in their places by their smarter offspring.

That, of course, is only one small part of the TV and movie scene. There are less subtle corrupting influences everywhere: violence, explicit sex, and most destructive of all, the linking of the two.

Dr. William Thorn, associate professor of journalism at Marquette University, has been observing the media scene for years. As a researcher and a father raising children in our media-saturated society, he has some strong opinions both about the destructive messages TV and movies send to our children and what parents can do to moderate their influence.

"There are really two major destructive influences—in addition to the obvious ones, explicit violence and sexuality—that you see in the media," Dr. Thorn says. "First, there's a very subtle undermining of parental control and maturity that elevates the child to the point of independence and self-sufficiency, making the parents' role much more difficult."

In too many television programs and movies, parents are held up for ridicule or are the butt of the jokes, rather than the source of moral authority. "I'm not referring to military-strict parents," Dr. Thorn is quick to point out. "I'm talking about parents who assert a reasonable amount of parental authority and whom the children respect because they have earned it. I think there are few TV programs in which that pattern exists."

Indeed, TV sitcoms present the father as a bumbling fool while the mother holds the family together and the children always know best, Dr. Thorn says. "I think this rise of superior, all-knowing, wise children who have to put up with incompetent parents is one of the very subtle messages that undermines not just parental authority but also respect for all those who are older," Dr. Thorn says. "That includes any status that grandparents might have as sources of knowledge or as authority figures. They are all dismissed as 'old-fashioned.' "

A second destructive message, according to Dr. Thorn, concerns materialism, which is often linked with youth. To be young, affluent, and have many possessions is held up as the ideal. It runs through nearly every teen-oriented show or commercial.

The culture of materialism is deeply embedded in all American media. They present an intensely competitive, money-oriented, success-oriented, beauty-oriented world. There's no call for teamwork. Instead there's a celebration of the individual, who is often against everybody else, to the point where the common good is denigrated.

Certainly kids are at risk to absorb many of the values the media plug. "One of the consolations from research in this area, though, is that a single exposure is not going to harm kids," Dr. Thorn says. "But one of the challenges is that unless you as a parent assert your parental role as the carrier of values to your children, TV will take it away from you."

Research shows that parents always have the most influence over their children's values—if they choose to use it. But if parents park their kids in front of the TV set, where they watch programs totally immune from any parental influence, uninterrupted destructive messages flood in.

Dr. Thorn cites a research study done several years

ago on the effect of television on adolescents' moral judgment. The researchers showed a group of teens TV programs and asked them to judge the rightness or wrongness of certain sexual behaviors. Then the researchers divided the kids into two groups. One group saw 15 hours of television clips from soap operas dealing with sexual situations. The other group watched innocuous fare. After the TV exposures, the groups were again tested on value judgments. The group that had seen the sexually explicit clips was much less likely to judge sexual behaviors as wrong than was the control group.[1]

"That led the researchers to conclude that prolonged exposure to programs of that sort reduces moral sensitivity to wrongness of infidelity and casual sex," Dr. Thorn says. Other studies with the same results have been done on the effects of watching violence.

If such a weakening of values can happen with just one week of intensive exposure, what happens to children who absorb hours of television every day? Research indicates that there are two types of television viewers. One type, in sociology jargon, is called "instrumental users." These people use television for a particular purpose: to get certain information, to take a limited break, for a half hour's entertainment with a particular program. In contrast there are "ritual users" who sit in front of the television no matter what's on, watching just to watch.

Instrumental users, research shows, are much less influenced by what they see because they put TV in a different perspective. They are not nearly as likely to see it as an alternate reality. Children whose parents have communicated clearly and consistently their standards of right and wrong are also less likely to be influenced by media values.

"When you have those two coming together—children who have been taught to use TV selectively and whose parents have communicated their values clearly and consistently—you have children who are more resistant to the messages the media are sending," Dr. Thorn says.

Which leads to what parents can do to blunt the influence of the media since it's probably not practical to prevent kids from viewing movies or TV. Dr. Thorn has several suggestions.

- **Watch television *with* your children.**
- **Teach them to select programs.** Sit down with the weekly listing and schedule what programs you are going to watch.
- **When choosing programs, ask questions.** "Why should we watch this program? Is there anything worth watching in it?"

These steps will make children instrumental rather than ritual users of television. Then:

- **Make sure your values come through loud and clear.** If there's violence in a program, ask, "That must have hurt a lot; how do you think that person felt?" Don't be afraid to say, "That would not be acceptable in our house because ..."
- **Be as careful with commercials and promotions for movies and upcoming shows as with the shows you choose to watch.** "That's tougher

because it's hit and run," Dr. Thorn says. Again, make it clear that certain behaviors are unacceptable to you.

- **With older children, you must speak as an adult to an adolescent, not as an adult to a child.** Ask, "What do you think about that person's behavior? What do your friends think about it? Do you agree with them?" You want your voice to echo in their ears.

- **Name actions for what they are.** "That's adultery. It's wrong. He's stealing. That's murder, they're wrong." That will reduce the glamour and appeal of the behaviors.

- **Teach your children to see what is going on underneath the surface of a program, to look for subtle messages.** That may mean asking them what they think a character was really saying or what his motivation was. It may mean provoking an argument about whether something is acceptable behavior or not. Teach your children to name what they are seeing. You can be sure the behaviors will not be named for what they are in the program.

- **Don't allow your children to watch TV in isolation.** That makes it impossible for you to interact with them and counteract the values portrayed on the show. Watching together and discussing the program also lessens the narcotic aspect of TV. Instead of vegetating in front of the TV, your children must think about what they are watching. If you do leave children alone to watch while you do a chore (TV *is* great while you're getting dinner!), be sure you know what the program is.

- **Don't get a child a TV set for his or her bedroom.** That's asking for unrestricted viewing.
- **Be especially vigilant if you subscribe to cable.** Many cable channels run unedited R-rated movies and syndicated series. You can buy devices to lock out certain channels when you're not home.
- **Even though movie viewing can be harder to control, make sure you read the reviews and know the rating of the movie your children want to see.** Dr. Thorn absolutely forbids R-rated movies for his children before age 18 and is very careful to read reviews of PG-13 films. He isn't afraid to say, "No, you can't go" or "No, you can't rent that video."
- **Discuss a movie your children have seen.** Ask what it was about. Ask if there was anything they found objectionable. If your children know that something in a film would upset you, then you've done your job. They've been sensitized and can see what's wrong for themselves.
- **Get a sense of the values of your children's friends.** Asking your kids what their friends thought of a movie or TV show allows you to assess the atmosphere in which they spend a lot of their time. Remember, during adolescence, friends' values become extremely important.
- **With older adolescents avoid the "I have power and you don't" scenario.** You want to make older teens intelligent consumers who are able to judge

the worth of things for themselves. It might be helpful to base discussions on external sources such as newspaper reviews or magazine articles. Teach kids to use these tools to guide their choices.

- **If you discover your children are watching objectionable movies or TV programs at a friend's house, you have a difficult problem.** Use the same process. Ask your children what they thought about the program. Then ask "What do you think I would have thought about it?" That forces your children to apply your values to what they saw. Dealing with the other parents can be tricky. Some parents don't see anything harmful in allowing their children to watch whatever they want, and they may consider you hopelessly old-fashioned and overprotective. You may have to say, "My child cannot watch a movie at your house without express permission from us." It will probably chill the relationship, but you have to draw the line. Be careful that you don't say, "You are wrong." Instead say, "I don't want this for my child." You might share some of the research with the other parents.

Dr. Thorn does not consider parents to be overly strict if they have rules about media viewing. "I don't think you can be overprotective," he says. "The research evidence is too clear. You show an 8- or 9-year-old an explicit sexual or violent scene and you have put an image in his or her head that may never go away. You don't know what the outcome of that will be."

While we've concentrated largely on the negative aspects of media, remember that there are positive aspects also. It probably wouldn't be a good idea to throw out the TV or lock the theater doors. Television can open windows for children and give them a great deal of information about the world, as well as some positive experiences. It all depends on how you use it.

But *you* must be in charge. If you aren't, you can be sure that Bart Simpson will be.

Further Reading
Anker, Roy M., et al., *Dancing in the Dark: Youth, Popular Culture, and the Electronic Media.* Grand Rapids: William B. Eerdmans Publishing Company, 1990.

Zillmann, Dolf, et al., editors. *Media, Children, and the Family: Social Scientific, Psychodynamic, and Clinical Perspective.* Hillsdale, New Jersey: Lawrence Erlbaum and Associates, Inc., 1994.

Notes
1. Dolf Zillmann, Jennings Bryant, and Steven Rockwell, "Effects of Massive Exposure to Sexually Explicit Television Fare on Adolescents' Moral Judgment." Testimony before the Attorney General's Committee on Pornography.

3

Mute Rock's Raucous Message

> *"Rock music gave me a way out. It gave me the right to drink, to take drugs. After all, who didn't want me to do those things? My parents, my teachers, that's who. And the music said, very bluntly, the heck with them—what are they doing for you?"*

So says Drew Faustmann, a young man who at age 22 has built his life around rock music. He's also dropped out of school twice, been through chemical dependency treatment three times, drifted far from God, and seen his dream of playing guitar with a rock band burned to ashes in the flames of rock's values.

"I believe rock music is just a commercial for a lifestyle," Faustmann says. "A commercial for 'do drugs, have sex with as many people as you can, don't take any lip from anybody, get money, and rule the world.'"

Kids are paying attention to that commercial, more attention than adults realize. Peter G. Christenson and Donald F. Roberts of the Carnegie Council on Adolescent Development surveyed younger teens, ages 11 to 15, to see how music influences them. They found kids this age spend four to five hours a day tuned in.

Kids listen to music for a variety of reasons: 91 percent reported listening "to pass the time," 83 percent to "relieve tension," and 79 percent to "handle moods." The stress of teen relationships shows up in the 67 percent who listen to "not feel so lonely" or the 62 percent who use music to "get in a certain mood with other people." Over half, 58 percent, listen to music to "think about what the lyrics mean."[1] You'll see how frightening that is as we explore what some lyrics say.

Most parents have no idea what their kids are absorbing when, headphoned or closeted behind bedroom doors, they turn up the volume and immerse themselves in their favorite group. Beyond hollering, "Turn down that music!" most of us are clueless as to why kids like that awful noise.

"The nature of the music and the images associated with it are so outrageous and offensive that parents often ignore it, believing it's just a phase their kids are going through. But every possible negative aspect of life is glorified, extolled, praised, and promoted in rock music," says Rev. John Spangler, who has spent decades studying rock music and gives seminars throughout the country on its dangers. "Many of the artists are involved in violent, anti-social lifestyles. They claim to be just reflecting our society—and in a sense they are reflecting the very worst elements in it—but in the process they *are* promoting it."

Are rock artists really trying to instill antisocial, anti-Christian values in young people? Or are they just playing up to an image to sell records? Listen to what some artists say and judge for yourself.

> "I figured that the only thing to do was steal their kids. I'm not talking about kidnapping. I'm just talking about changing young people's value systems which removes them from their parents' world very effectively." (David Crosby of Crosby, Stills and Nash, as quoted in an interview in Rolling Stone.)[2]
>
> "We're back to destroy your minds and you know we're destroying your minds and you love it." (Note on the cover of the KISS album "Destroyer.")
>
> "To manipulate children's minds in religion or politics would raise a storm of outrage, protest and legislation, but in the field of commerce children are fair game." (Note on the cover of the album "Welcome to the Pleasure Dome" by Frankie Goes to Hollywood, which features art suggesting oral sex and bestiality.)

Today's rock music promotes things—rebellion, hate, violence (especially toward women), twisted sexuality, drug and alcohol use, suicide, the occult—that would appall parents and make them furious if they knew.

To walk through the world of rock is not an easy trip. The images presented in lyrics and album art are so distasteful that you want to turn away and avoid dealing with them. The images are also difficult to write about because so much is too obscene to quote in a Christian publication. But look at it we must, if we want to save our children from its destructive influence. Come with me on this unpleasant journey.

Rebellion

One of the major themes in rock music is rebellion. Singers shake their fists at parental authority, the authority of the state, and God's authority. "It's power-driven music, and it's about hating," Faustmann says.

Elton John sings in "Bennie and the Jets":

> *"Let's take ourselves along, where we fight our parents out in the streets to find out who's right and who's wrong."*

The video for the song "We're Not Going to Take It" by Twisted Sister portrays a young boy listening to rock music. He's corrected by his father and then turns into the lead singer of the rock group. His brothers and sisters become the rest of the band, and they beat their father, throw him down a flight of stairs, and toss him out an upstairs window.

Police officers, the ultimate symbols of authority, are often marked for death in rock lyrics, especially by gangsta rap groups. Rapper Ice-T caused a public protest over his song, "Cop Killer," which forced Time Warner to remove it from the album. Another gangsta rap group, NWA, has a song called "F—— the Police."

Violence

Rock music is saturated with and dominated by violence. References to murder, rape, and torture abound. "They're singing about beating to a pulp anyone who doesn't agree with you," Faustmann says.

The Grammy-nominated band Suicidal Tendencies

has a song titled "I Saw Your Mommy and Your Mommy's Dead," which includes graphic descriptions of chopped off feet and rats nesting in her hair. The gangsta rap group The Geto Boys sings about getting a girl "ready and sweaty" and then slicing her up with a machete until her guts are like spaghetti.

A very popular group, Guns 'n Roses, (their symbol is two guns entwined with roses) has a song titled "I Used to Love Her But I Had to Kill Her." The name of the group Iron Maiden refers to a spike-studded body case used for torture. The cover of their "Killer" album depicts one of the singers hacking someone with a bloody axe. Dave Mustaine of the group Megadeth, in an interview in the magazine *Faces,* said, "We're political and *violent* and sexual and drug-oriented and educational and fun" (emphasis added).[3]

Violence in rock has reached new heights in the music videos featured on MTV, a widely available, 24-hour-a-day cable station whose average viewer is 15 years old. The National Coalition on Television Violence analyzed the content of 750 music videos and found they averaged more than 20 acts of violence per hour.[4] Just one example: The video for "Poundcake" by Van Halen shows a group of women using a power drill to bore out the eye of someone watching them through a keyhole.

The violent image some rock groups portray on stage sometimes reflects their personal lives. In the past two years, several rappers and rock stars have been arrested for violent behavior, including murder, carjacking, and physical abuse. Kids have a tough time separating the image and the music. The insanity on stage, the driving music, and kids who can't control their actions have caused some concerts to turn into riots.

Sexual Messages

"The word *love* in rock music means *sex*," warns Rev. Spangler. " 'Let me love you all night long' doesn't mean 'Let's have an interpersonal emotional relationship until the sun comes up!' "

Rev. Spangler points out that every kind of sex is condoned and promoted: heterosexual, homosexual, incest, rape, sex with animals, sex linked with torture and brutality. "Women are portrayed as sex objects to be exploited, as people who enjoy being brutalized," he says.

Sex has always been one of rock's main messages, even in the early days. In 1967, Andrew Oldham, then manager of the Rolling Stones, was quoted in *Time* as saying, "Rock music is sex and you have to hit them in the face with it."[5] By today's standards the sexual images Oldham was thinking about were mild, cloaked in double entendre. No longer. Today's images are a raw, brutal slap in the face.

I apologize for the words and images in this section, but it isn't enough to tell you that rock music is filled with crude language and sexual references. Unless you actually read some of it for yourself, you can have no concept of how far it has gone and what sexual messages rock groups are pouring into the minds of impressionable kids, some as young as 10 or 12.

The musician formerly known as Prince sings about 23 positions in a one-night stand and describes quite a few of them—on the kitchen floor, in the bathtub, or on the pool table. The video features blindfolded women led into an orgy of unclothed bodies squirming in ecstasy. He also praises incest in his song "Sister." In yet another song, he sings about deflowering a virgin in a river of blood.

Some images are raw and violent. NWA in "Findum, F— um and Flee" sings in the coarsest street language about open female genitals, male genitals raw from intercourse, and orders to the "bitch" for oral sex. Women in rap are routinely referred to as either "bitch" or "ho" meaning whore. The group, 2 Live Crew chimes in with a song instructing a woman to "Suck my d—, nibble on my d— like a rat does cheese."

MTV is the sex-pushers' heaven because erotic visual images can multiply the power of the verbal message many times over. Thus Janet Jackson's love song may have mild words, but the image of her in lacy underwear with a man stroking and kissing her body is anything but mild. Dr. Bradley Greenberg, a researcher at Michigan State University, concluded that watching just one hour of MTV per day would expose a teen to 1,500 video sex experiences every year.[6]

The celebration of perverted sexual acts has become so extreme that even some people in the music industry are becoming disillusioned. Joni Mitchell, a singer and composer, said in an interview in *Rolling Stone*, "Every generation has to be more shocking than the last. But at a certain point you've got to reel it in because ... our country is going down the tubes from it. It's rotten to the core."[7]

Along with promoting extreme promiscuity, several groups also include pro-abortion messages. Artists allied with a group called Rock for Choice know how to influence kids. Exene Cervenka, a singer from the group X, said in *Rolling Stone*, "(When kids see) people they really respect and love speaking out on [abortion], it becomes part of the experience, and they accept it with the music." L7 guitarist Donita Sparks said in the same interview, "We didn't want to preach to the converted. We wanted to get people who would be affected by abortion laws the most: young kids."[8]

Drugs and Alcohol

Since the days when the Beatles sang about LSD under the title "Lucy in the Sky with Diamonds," rock music has been as much of a drug pusher as the street peddler. It's little different today.

Use of any kind of chemical is glorified in rock groups. You never see Axl Rose, lead singer of Guns 'n Roses, without a bottle of whiskey in his hand. Rumor has it that many rock groups' alcohol bottles really contain herbal tea, but even if true, that doesn't excuse them for promoting alcohol use to fans well under legal drinking age.

The drug references in today's rock songs have become more sophisticated and hidden. They go over parents' heads because they use slang terms unfamiliar to most adults. When a group sings about Panama, how many parents know that's marijuana? Or that Mr. Brownstone is heroin? Or that the famous strawberry fields refers to speed?

Even if, as rock musicians claim, drug references have declined since the heyday of the psychedelic '60s, the lifestyles of the musicians themselves are an advertisement for drug and alcohol use. Many rock stars are known users, a lot of them have been through chemical abuse treatment, and a significant number have died from drug overdoses. That doesn't seem to stop groups like KISS from singing songs such as "Mr. Speed" or "Mainline" (about injecting drugs) or a group with the biblical-sounding name Nazareth from recording a song titled "Cocaine."

Religion and the Occult

It's not surprising that rock groups mock Christianity at every turn. After all, God's Word speaks out loudly and clearly against their promiscuous, hedonistic, and irresponsible lifestyles. As a result, anything that has to do with Christ or any Christian church—including the Bible, ministers, nuns, priests, and Christian symbols—has taken knocks. The group Slayer sings, "I can take your lost soul from the grave. Jesus knows your soul cannot be saved. Crucify the so-called Lord." George Michael, on his album misnamed "Faith," states that he doesn't need the Bible, just sex. Or there's Ozzy Osbourne smashing a cross to the floor.

If rock artists hate Christianity, they certainly flirt with Satan worship. Album covers abound with occult symbols and many songs glorify Satan. Perhaps, as some suspect, only a few rock artists really believe in Satanism and the rest hint at it only to boost sales. That hypocrisy doesn't excuse them. "If they are only doing it for money, that's the worst reason of all," says Rev. Spangler. "They don't care how it's affecting kids, kids who take them seriously even if they're not. That's totally irresponsible."

Suicide

The rate of suicide among teens has skyrocketed more than 300 percent in the last few decades. Suicide is one of the leading causes of death among high school students. When you consider that a percentage of the deaths listed as car accidents and drug overdoses might not be accidental, suicide could leap to the top of the list. The subject of suicide references in rock music is controversial. Many psychologists support the contention of rock groups that music doesn't cause a person to commit suicide. And certainly we can't prove that it does. We can, however, say that a young person who is depressed can easily find the message in rock music that suicide is okay, a solution to problems. "People who are looking for permission to blow themselves away will hear it in rock music," says Rev. Spangler.

Elton John sings about buying a .45 and giving them all a surprise. "Think I'm gonna kill myself, cause a little suicide," he sings. Nirvana had a song titled "I Hate Myself and Want to Die." The group's lead singer, Kurt Cobain, killed himself with a shotgun.

Rock groups, notably Judas Priest, have been sued by parents, claiming their music influenced their children to commit suicide. Even if music doesn't have that kind of power, common sense has to ask if listening to music that pours death messages into a young person's mind is healthy.

You've survived the trip through the world of rock music. Do you feel dirty? I know I did after spending hours reading rock lyrics and interviews with rock stars.

If you didn't realize how bad the rock scene has become, your initial reaction is probably, "Someone should stop them!" But in our country with its First Amendment protection, that's not easy to do. Nor is it necessarily desirable. In a free country even the most odious speech is protected. It's dangerous to put the power of censorship into the government's hands.

What *can* you do? Your first priority as a parent must be to protect your kids. Just as you wouldn't permit them to take poison, you must stop rock music from poisoning their souls. If enough parents do that, and enough kids join in, declining sales dollars will force rock music to clean up its act. (Remind your teen that every time he or she buys an album by an objectionable artist, it puts money in that person's pocket.)

The first step in the battle, though, is to become informed. Vague speeches to your kids that you've heard rock music is bad won't have any effect. You need to know what you are talking about. As unpleasant as that may be, it means you've got to read the lyrics to rock songs (easier than trying to understand them through the music!). Many albums include lyric sheets, and rock magazines sometimes print the words to the latest hits. (Your library probably carries *Rolling Stone* and some of the other rock magazines.) Listen to your local rock station and spend a few hours watching MTV. Once armed with the facts, you'll be ready to talk to your teen. Start by praying. You'll need God's help and guidance, which He promises to give you.

According to Rev. Spangler, forbidding your child to listen to rock music without any justification, especially if he or she is already heavily involved, may make it more attractive—the old forbidden fruit effect. "Every kid who asks the question 'why' deserves a studied answer, one that's as complete as possible," he says. "You have to show respect for them. Showing disrespect is one of the quickest ways to have them reject your advice."

Rev. Spangler suggests sitting down with your teen and listening to the music together, following along with the printed words if possible. Study the album covers and posters. Ask your child's opinions as well as expressing your own. Zero in on specific references or images you find objectionable and ask, "Is this God-pleasing? Knowing Jesus is here, sitting on the bed with you, do you feel comfortable with this line? This image?" Listen, discuss, don't lecture. Your goal is to teach your child discernment. You want him or her to come to the conclusion that much of rock music is a bad influence and then make the decision to turn away.

Should you, after exploring the music with your teen, forbid what you find objectionable? That's a very personal decision say Dan and Steve Peters, authors of *Why Knock Rock?* (a book on the dangers of rock music). The answer depends on a lot of factors, including your child's age (with younger children more parental control is appropriate), the depth of his or her involvement with the music, and whether or not you think your child is at risk for drinking, drugs, suicide, or promiscuity. Remember that you can't insulate your teenager completely—rock music is in the school cafeteria, at friends' houses, and in the shopping mall.

Rev. Spangler took a tough line with his own kids. They weren't allowed to listen to certain music. Fortunately they came to agree with him, and today, as young adults, they assist with his anti-rock seminars.

If a child rebels you have a harder task. Rev. Spangler thinks in that case you should resort to anything necessary to turn your child away from evil. "I see parents who are about to lose their kids, and they give in to this stuff. Rock music is raising their kids, and they end up a statistic," he says. "I would tell my kids, 'I have to give an account to God some day, and the answer is no.'"

You should also make it clear to your teenagers, say the Peters, that you are not condemning sex but the sexual perversion rock music celebrates; not honest questioning but rebellion. And don't make God the "bad guy" you hide behind by telling them they have to stop listening because God says so. Rather, take responsibility for your own feelings and help your kids explore God's will. Pray together, asking God to help your child make Christ-like choices.

Turning away from rock music will leave a void in your teen's life. Your other task as a concerned parent is to provide an alternative. Fortunately there's some clean, decent secular rock music out there—you just have to look for it. And there's a whole world of Christian contemporary music. No matter what genre of music your kids like—top 40, heavy metal, rap—there's a Christian group doing it. And they're good, in many cases technically better than the secular groups. By the way, be careful with group names. A few secular groups have Christian-sounding names—Ministry is not a Christian group!

There are even Christian rock concerts with the

same excitement and quality of entertainment the secular groups offer but without the drugs, sex, and violence. My two kids attended a large outdoor Christian rock festival when they were younger. They came home sunburned and exhilarated in their faith, proudly reporting that in four days there hadn't been a single arrest. The police were astounded!

"Once they are convinced, your kids may be even more restrictive in what they will listen to than you are, and your policing activities may fall to a minimum," says Rev. Spangler. "Your kids are going to appreciate you for this. Maybe not right away, but they will!"

Drew Faustmann has really walked through the valley of rock. "It took me to the bottom," he says. "I've done just about everything imaginable, and I've hurt a lot of people in the process. I'm very honest and open about that because I want people to learn from me."

Faustmann's getting his life together again. He's off drugs and alcohol, and he's back with God. He's going back to school, still in music but concentrating on jazz rather than rock. He wants to compose, perform, and teach. "As I grow more knowledgeable, I can see the messages (in rock)," Faustmann says. "As I'm getting back into God, I've started looking at that music to see what it was that I liked about it. It was that I could be talented, that I could get respect through it. These guys are very smart, they're good at their music, and they know what they're doing.

"But kids who follow this lifestyle are giving up everything, and that's why it's so horrible," Faustmann reflects sadly.

Further Reading

Peters, Dan, Steve Peters, and Cher Merrill. *Why Knock Rock?* Minneapolis: Bethany House Publishers, 1984.

Medved, Michael. *Hollywood vs. America: Popular Culture and the War Against Traditional Values.* New York: HarperCollins Publishers, 1992.

Notes

1. Jolene L. Roehlkepartain, "Why Music Matters so Much to Your Kids," *Jr. High Ministry* (November/December 1991): 4.
2. Dan Peters, Steve Peters, and Cher Merrill, *Why Knock Rock?*, (Minneapolis: Bethany House Publishers, 1984), 96.
3. Quoted in Rev. John Spangler, "Rock Music: Quotes and Lyrics," (n. p.).
4. Michael Medved, *Hollywood vs. America: Popular Culture and the War Against Traditional Values*, (New York: HarperCollins Publishers, 1992), 192.
5. Peters, et al., 67.
6. Medved, 245.
7. Quoted in Medved, 104.
8. Kim Neely, "The Fight for the Right to Choose," *Rolling Stone* (March 18, 1993): 22.

4

Encourage Cross-cultural Education

And Understand the Myths of Multiculturalism

In the fifth-grade classroom, children learn about the contributions made to our society by Frederick Douglass, Martin Luther King Jr., Harriet Tubman, and other African-American leaders. Students listen to jazz and sample "soul food." Junior high literature students read stories by Native American, Asian, and women writers along with O. Henry and Mark Twain.

A healthy development in education? Certainly. Students need to know the contributions people from all races and both sexes have made to our country. Multiculturalism? Perhaps. Perhaps not. It depends on how you define the word.

Understanding Multiculturalism

To a lot of parents (and teachers too), *multiculturalism* means exposing children to many cultures and the contributions they have made to our common American heritage. That's a cause to support and celebrate. Some observers warn, however, that multiculturalism can also be a code word for a viewpoint that's destructive to our country, which promotes breaking down our society into competing ethnic groups.

Dr. Alvin Schmidt, professor of sociology at Illinois College in Jacksonville, Illinois, explains, "Teaching kids about other cultures isn't multiculturalism—it's simply education. If we have to label it, I would call it cross-cultural education."

Multiculturalism, on the other hand, has an *ism* in its name. "An *ism* is an ideology," Dr. Schmidt explains. "And this one is making deep inroads into our social institutions, including schools. If most people looked seriously at multiculturalism and understood what it means, they would run away from it."

What Does *Multiculturalism* Mean?

As part of defining the word, let's make it clear that teaching children to recognize—and celebrate—the contributions of all people, including those too-long ignored, is a good thing. All children—African-American, Caucasian, Asian, Native American, and Hispanic—are enriched by understanding and learning about each other. Borrowing Dr. Schmidt's term, cross-cultural education is healthy.

Ideological multiculturalism, to again borrow his term, is something quite different. Arthur Schlesinger Jr., one of our country's most respected historians, has written of the dangers of ideological multiculturalism in *The Disuniting of America*. Critics say that our way of teaching history has denied people heroes from their own ethnic groups, he writes. To remedy that, multiculturalism "became a cult, and today it threatens to become a counter-revolution against the original theory of America as one people, a common culture, a single nation."¹

Strong words? Yes. But in the view of many, ideological multiculturalism is a movement that teaches children to identify themselves primarily as African, Spanish, or Asian rather than American. It teaches minority children that they are victims of Western oppression. It teaches kids that no one culture's customs are any better, or any worse, than those of any other culture's.

Linda Chavez, writing in *The National Review*, put it this way:

> *"In the past, government—especially public schools—saw it as a duty to try to bring newcomers into the fold by teaching them English, by introducing them to the great American heroes as their own, by instilling respect for American institutions. Lately, we have nearly reversed course, treating each group, new and old, as if what is most important is to preserve its separate identity and space."*²

Where does the ideological multiculturalist viewpoint come from? Richard Bernstein, a reporter for the *New York Times*, says in his book *Dictatorship of Virtue: Multiculturalism and the Battle for America's Future* that ideological multiculturalism is "a movement of the left, emerging from the counterculture of the 1960s." It is, he says, the sliding of the Civil Rights movement into fanaticism or dogmatism.³

What are the dangers in ideological multiculturalism? Dr. Schmidt concentrates on three.

1. **The tendency of ideological multiculturalists to encourage people to see themselves first as part of a racial or ethnic group and second as Americans.** There's certainly nothing wrong with encouraging children to take pride in their ethnic backgrounds and to observe, if they wish, the customs of their ancestral culture. But that's quite different from teaching kids to see themselves as primarily Africans, Mexicans, or Chinese rather than as Americans.

   Stressing cultural heritage first can lead to excesses that hurt the very minorities it's intended to help. For example, some educators say you shouldn't teach children to become fluent in English but encourage them, as a matter of ethnic pride, to speak their native language or a variation of English such as black English. But reality states that you cannot climb the ladder of economic success in this country without being fluent in English. "Can you imagine Colin Powell becoming a Joint Chief of Staff if he spoke black English?" asks Dr. Schmidt. "To ask the question is to answer it."

2. **The tendency of the ideological multiculturalist to rewrite history to make minorities feel better—sort of "history as therapy."** One example is the statement, now included in many American history textbooks, that the United States Constitution was based on the political system of the Iroquois Indians. Schlesinger calls Iroquois influence "marginal to the point of invisibility."[5] Dr. Schmidt calls the statement "very bad history."

Rewriting history is dangerous no matter the motivation, Dr. Schmidt says. "That was the method the Soviets used—rewrite the encyclopedias and history books to suit your political views. It's revisionism of the worst kind," he adds.

3. **In ideological multiculturalism, children are subtly taught that there is no objective standard of right and wrong, that it all depends on your culture.** To a true ideological multiculturalist, Western values, for example, cannot be held up as a model; safe-guarding individual human rights is no better than socialism. Only different.

Relative truth in matters of morality is a viewpoint Christians cannot accept. We have an unchanging standard of right and wrong: God's Word. Cultural practices that fly in the face of God's commands are not just "different," they are wrong. In a recent survey of college students done by Students for America, only 38 percent of those surveyed said they believe right and wrong are not a matter of personal opinion and that there are indeed absolutes.[6] That's frightening. Thanks to God's renewing work in our Baptism, we live as His children. Talk with your children about the forgiveness and refreshment we receive each time we receive the Lord's Supper. Through Word and Sacrament, God's Holy Spirit gives us the means to walk with Christ.

Recognizing Ideological Multiculturalism

How can a parent know if his or her child is being taught cross-cultural education in school or if ideological multiculturalism is creeping in? Bernstein writes about an elementary school student in Massachusetts who came home from school and asked his mother, "Why do they teach us that white people suck?"[7] Ignoring the crude language, if your child asks a similar question, you've got a pretty good clue as to what's going on!

Dr. Schmidt suggests that parents look closely at their children's textbooks, especially those used for history and social studies. He points out several "red flags."

- **How is Christianity treated?** In ideological texts, it's either omitted or bad-mouthed. "[Ideological] texts will never mention any contribution Christianity has made to civilization but will bend over backward to credit other cultures or even fabricate their contributions," Dr. Schmidt says. "For example, many books ignore the fact that slavery was opposed first and foremost by Christian leaders. The same is true of the role of Christians in the Civil Rights movement. Many texts conveniently forget that Martin Luther King Jr. was a Christian minister and that many Civil Rights workers came from church groups." Most importantly, textbooks will never present the truth of God's inspired Word and the atoning sacrifice of God's Son, the Word Incarnate. God calls on us, as parents, to nurture our children in His Word.

- **Look for bias in the presentation of other cultures.** Ideological texts will often write glowingly of the great civilizations of the Aztecs and Mayans, for example, but never mention that they engaged in ritual human sacrifice. They also sometimes omit the fact that slavery existed among American Indians before Columbus and was practiced in some areas of Africa until the 1980s. "Multiculturalism is a biased presentation," Dr. Schmidt says, "leaving out the bad things from other cultures and the good things from our own. That's not honest history. All cultures, including ours, should be taught honestly—the bad with the good."

- **Read between the lines for content that makes morality and truth seem relative.** It won't be stated directly but subtly suggested in statements about how what we consider right may not be right in another culture. Christians cannot accept that. God has set standards of right and wrong that do not change. We walk, not in the way of the world, but in the footsteps of our Savior.

- **Watch for buzz words like *oppression* and *racism*.** Did oppression and racism exist in our history? Beyond a doubt. Does racism still exist today? No thinking person could deny it. Racism and oppression of other people, such as African Americans and Native Americans, should not be excused or covered up. But if a textbook dwells on these issues and excludes everything positive about Western culture, then it is not painting an accurate picture. The textbook is moving toward what

Bernstein calls "that familiar skid into ideological excess, into education as compensation for past wrongs, the curriculum as expiation for guilt ... a worm gnawing away at any notion of American goodness."[8]

Protecting Your Child

If you feel your child's school is sliding into ideological multiculturalism rather than cross-cultural education, what can you do? Here, too, Dr. Schmidt has some suggestions.

- **Inform yourself and other parents of what's being taught.** Then meet with school officials and tell them how you feel. You may be labeled "Christian-right censors," but you also may be able to affect change.

- **If nothing is done and you have no other school option, you can "inoculate" your child by talking with him or her.** Point out the bias in the textbook. Make sure your child knows that in America we enjoy a degree of individual liberty and an emphasis on human rights that people in other countries envy. If moral relativism is suggested, ask your child what God thinks about that. Would God agree that people decide for themselves what is right and wrong? Kids whose parents are there to guide them can see through this stuff.

When discussing slavery and the treatment of Native Americans in our history, don't try to hide or sugarcoat the truth. Tell your child, "Human beings are sinful, and we have done sinful things in our country." But balance it with the truth about individuals and groups that worked to end slavery and bring about civil rights for minorities. "You must teach children both sides of a cultural experience," says Dr. Schmidt.

- **Prepare your child to take some flack if he or she expresses opinions in the classroom that go against multicultural America-bashing.** On the other hand, you might be surprised to find teachers are quite sympathetic. "I would argue that the average teacher doesn't understand ideological multiculturalism but is perceptive enough to realize that much of what is being taught is slanted," Dr. Schmidt says. "It often isn't the teachers bringing in this stuff, it's the higher-ups at the state and national level."

Your own Christian attitude toward other races and cultures is the most important influence on your children. Model the belief that God loves all people equally, that He sent His Son to die for the sins of everyone regardless of race or culture, and that through Jesus' death and resurrection we are all one ("There is neither Jew nor Greek, slave nor free, male nor female, for you are all one in Christ Jesus." Galatians 3:28). Help your children see all people as God's children who need salvation in His Son, regardless of race. That's the true basis for healthy cross-cultural education.

Further Reading

Bernstein, Richard. *Dictatorship of Virtue: Multiculturalism and the Battle for America's Future.* New York: Alfred A. Knopf, Inc., 1994.

Schlesinger, Jr., Arthur M., *The Disuniting of America.* New York: W. W. Norton and Company, Inc., 1992.

Notes

1. Arthur M. Schlesinger Jr., *The Disuniting of America*, (New York: W. W. Norton and Company, Inc., 1992): 43.
2. Linda Chavez, "Demystifying Multiculturalism," *The National Review* (February 21, 1994): 32.
3. Richard Bernstein, *Dictatorship of Virtue: Multiculturalism and the Battle for America's Future,* (New York: Alfred A. Knopf, Inc., 1994): 6, 9.
4. Schlesinger, 35.
5. Ibid, 77.
6. Cal Thomas, from his column titled, "The Truth about Higher Learning in America."
7. Bernstein, 235.
8. Ibid, 278.

5

Uncover the Problems of Promiscuity

The soft-spoken, gray-haired pediatrician stared at the phone on the corner of his desk as though it were a snake. "I hate to make this call," he said.

"Hello, Tricia? This is Dr. Eagleton. The results of your test are back. I'm sorry to tell you this, but you have a sexually transmitted disease. It's called chlamydia. Have you had sex recently? Prom night? I see. Well, you're going to have to get treatment. And you'll have to tell your date. He'll need treatment too."

I was sitting in the pediatrician's office, shadowing him for the afternoon as part of a medical journalists' intern program. Dr. Eagleton (not his real name) leaned back in his chair, took off his glasses, and rubbed his eyes wearily. "I didn't used to have to make that kind of call to 15-year-olds," he said in frustration.

Our society has changed enormously in its attitude toward sex in the last three decades. Not that there wasn't sexual activity among young people in the past—there certainly was. But it wasn't as common, it wasn't expected, it wasn't considered to be the normal way for teenagers to behave. And sex wasn't celebrated in the media with couples engaging in intimate, behind-closed-bedroom-door acts in living color on movie and TV screens.

What caused this shift in sexual values? Theorists offer many answers: The revolution against all values that erupted during the '60s. The breakdown of the family and religious institutions that resulted. The increasing use of sex in the media and advertising to make money. An "I can be even more outrageous than you" mentality on the part of film and television producers. The subtle putdown of traditional sexual values among the so-called cultural elite, who mock "Ozzie-and-Harriet" families and chastise those who espouse monogamy and chastity as "intolerant right-wingers" who just aren't with it.

Kids grow up steeped in that cultural brew. From their friends they get the message, "If you want to be one of the 'in crowd,' you've got to do it." Sex education courses in schools may tell them "Only you can make the decision when to be sexually active, and as long as you use a condom, it's okay." Even the United States surgeon general said we've got to start teaching kids what to do in the backseat of a car.

Amidst this overwhelming chorus, the voice of parents and the church calls out, "God says to wait." But it can seem still, small, and easily drowned out.

Kids are the ones who have paid an enormous price for our country's confusion about sexuality and its preaching of open sexual expression. Studies show that American kids are becoming sexually active at ever earlier ages. A survey done by the Minneapolis-based Search Institute polled 46,000 sixth- through twelfth-graders who lived in Midwestern communities under 100,000 in population. Research found that within this probably more-conservative-than-average group, 30 percent had had sexual intercourse. And this group included *sixth graders!* Surveys done with high school kids have found rates of sexual activity as high as 60 or 70 percent.

Despite the media's preaching that free sexuality is good, American kids have paid a steep price in horrendous rates of sexually transmitted diseases and teen pregnancy.

Sex is good. Let's make no mistake about that. God gave it to us and what He gives is always good. But He also gave us an "owner's manual" on how to use our bodies. Kids need to learn that. They need to learn that early sexual experimentation and promiscuity carry with them severe consequences, both emotional and physical.

"The biggest emotional consequence of teen sex is the damage it does to self-esteem," says Linda McClintock, a therapist with a Christian counseling agency that has extensive experience running support and therapy groups for teens.

What teens usually say, she reports, is that there was a side of them that didn't want to have sex. They feel they weren't true to that side. "Early adolescents often get 'sucked into' the heat of the moment," McClintock says. "Their friends are saying 'I've done it and it's okay,' so they aren't true to their own values."

Afterward teenagers often feel they have become

an object for someone else's use, McClintock says, especially if the relationship was brief. "Girls often say, 'He said he loved me and he'd stay with me, but then he was gone,' " she says. "They feel used and that damages them emotionally."

While girls may own up to their emotional pain more readily, boys suffer too. Some say they feel tremendous pressure from their peers to "be a man." Some boys are talked into sex by girls, McClintock says. "He may be afraid to say no for fear he'll be laughed at. Guys often think it's just a physical thing and then are surprised by their emotional reaction," she says.

Beside the emotional pain, there is often a physical price to be paid for sexual activity. Dr. Debra Schaeffer is an obstetrician/gynecologist and a Christian. Her practice includes quite a few young women. "I'm seeing more sexually active girls, at a younger age," she says. "When I was in training the youngest girls we would see would be 15 or 16, but now we're seeing them as early as 12, 13, or 14."

She finds the trend distressing because she, like Dr. Eagleton, has to take care of the consequences. Sexually transmitted diseases (abbreviated as STDs) are on the rise in her practice. Dr. Schaeffer says teens are often unaware of the profound consequences that can come from being infected by one of these bugs.

There are more than 20 different infections that can be passed from person to person during sex (some of them, such as AIDS, can also be acquired in other ways). Some STDs are caused by treatable bacteria and can be cured with antibiotics. Some are the result of viruses and can't be cured with antibiotics, although their symptoms often can be treated.

While contracting an STD is no picnic for men, the consequences for women are even more severe. Not only can women become infected more easily, they suffer much more serious after-effects if the infection goes untreated.

Many STDs, Dr. Schaeffer says, can result in pelvic inflammatory disease (PID), a raging abdominal infection that can involve the uterus, fallopian tubes, ovaries, or other abdominal organs. "The infection can cause adhesions, or scars, to form. If that happens in the [fallopian] tubes, they can close off, causing infertility," she says.

The most prevalent STDs teens should know about are:

- **Chlamydia.** The most common STD, chlamydia is caused by a bacteria that lives within human cells. It's transmitted only by sexual contact. When symptoms are present (often there are none), they include vaginal or penial discharge, burning during urination, and mild lower abdominal pain. Consequences include PID and pneumonia and eye infections in newborns. Chlamydia is treated with antibiotics.

- **Trichomoniasis.** This disease often produces no symptoms, especially in men. If symptoms do develop, they include a yellowish, foul-smelling discharge; genital irritation and itching; and burning during urination. Trich can cause premature labor, which may result in a premature birth if the labor is not stopped. It's treated with oral or vaginal antibiotics.

- **Gonorrhea.** "People generally know when they have this one," Dr. Schaeffer says. Symptoms include a pus-filled discharge and itching or burning during urination. Gonorrhea often leads to PID. It can cause blindness and meningitis in newborns. In men, gonorrhea can lead to strictures in the penis that require painful dilation with small tubes. It's usually cured with penicillin, but some strains are becoming resistant and harder to cure.
- **Human Papilloma Virus (HPV).** This virus causes warts on the genitals of both men and women, either internally or externally. In some women, the warts are believed to lead to cervical cancer. There is no cure because the cause is a virus, but the warts themselves can be burned off with a laser or acid or frozen off. If they become precancerous and have to be cut out, the operation may weaken the cervix (the entrance to the uterus) enough to put a woman at risk of premature delivery during the final months of her pregnancy.
- **Genital Herpes.** Caused by a virus, an infection with this disease results in outbreaks of very painful sores in the genital area. Subsequent outbreaks are likely to be less severe than the first one. Symptoms can be suppressed with an expensive drug called acyclovir, but the infection is not curable. "You have to learn to manage it and live with it," says Dr. Schaeffer.
- **Syphilis.** "It's not true that syphilis is a disease of days gone by," Dr. Schaeffer says. "It's a disease that's on its way back." The first sign of infection is a painless sore on the genitals that goes away. But

the infection has merely gone underground. Fever, sore throat, and a rash may come next. In later stages, the disease causes severe neurological damage, blindness, dementia, and death. Most babies born to infected women don't survive because of severe birth defects. Syphilis can be cured with penicillin, but the drug is becoming less effective as resistant strains develop.

- **Hepatitis B.** About half of the people infected with Hepatitis B show no symptoms. Others have a fever, head and muscle aches, fatigue, nausea, and yellowing of the eyes and skin. Hepatitis is caused by a virus. Most cases clear up without serious consequences, but some people become chronic carriers, which increases risk for liver cancer.

- **HIV/AIDS.** While AIDS has been portrayed as a disease contracted by homosexuals and drug users, it's increasingly being spread through heterosexual sex to young people. Those with the HIV virus can live for years without symptoms. Once AIDS develops, though, it wreaks havoc on the immune system, allowing other infections to run rampant. Inevitably the person dies. There are some drugs to decrease symptoms, but there is no cure. Thirty percent of babies born to infected mothers develop AIDS (if the mother takes the drug AZT, the rate is lower). Infected babies rarely live more than a few years.

Besides the physical effects of STDs, they also exact an emotional price, says McClintock. Shame, embarrassment, and a feeling of dirtiness are common. Girls, especially, worry they may have permanently damaged their bodies—a realistic fear. Most young girls are uncomfortable about having a gynecological exam, which may be necessary in some cases. For either a boy or a girl, it's humiliating to tell sexual partners that they may have been infected.

While STDs are a real risk in sexual activity, there's an even greater one: pregnancy. A pregnancy outside of marriage presents a young woman with three basic options, all of which carry enormous emotional pain.

Abortion should not be an option for Christian girls. Sadly, many Christian young women do consider abortions, and some even go through with the procedure. If a young girl has an abortion, she can experience severe guilt and needs God's message of forgiveness. A young woman can carry the baby to term and place her child for adoption, which means a different type of pain as she says good-bye. Or she can keep the baby, which often closes doors to education and normal teen life and may lock her into a lifetime of poverty.

If the young woman is in her early teens, pregnancy also may have physical consequences. "The pelvis isn't well-developed, which places a young girl at risk of premature delivery or C-section," explains Dr. Schaeffer. "The risk of birth defects is higher in mothers under age 15. We don't know why, it may be that her eggs aren't fully mature."

Parents know the dangers teen sexual activity presents. It's hard to live in our society and not see the consequences. What can you as a parent do to prevent your child from succumbing to the lure of "casual" sex?

First, kids have to be told what God says about the place of sexuality in His plan. They need to know that sexual desires are normal. "We are people who need relationships, who need cleaving, who need sex," Dr. Schaeffer says. "Everything in your body is driving you to a union with another person. God wouldn't have said it's not good for people to be alone if He didn't know that we need each other."

Second, they need to know that God says sex is to be part of a *married* relationship. We all have the ability to abuse God's gift of sexuality, and we need His power to resist that urge. Dr. Schaeffer recalls a study in which the few college seniors who were still virgins were asked why. "They found the number 1 reason was religious," she says. "The people I see in my practice who abstain from sex are those who believe that it's reserved for marriage by God's Law." She thinks it's important that kids get that message at home, in church, and through Bible study to counteract the messages in the media. As your children grow and mature, help them celebrate their sexuality as a gift from God. Remind them that as baptized children of God, the Holy Spirit will help them overcome sexual temptation, just as He helps them in all avenues of life with Christ.

McClintock thinks good communication within the family is another key. Kids need to feel they can ask any question, that there is no off-limits topic. Discuss the consequences of sex with your kids, point out any examples you know of in which people's lives were adversely affected by sexual promiscuity. Share information about STDs. Discuss the emotional effects as well as the physical.

McClintock also suggests setting limits. "I think curfews are a good idea," she says. "And whatever happened to the idea of no single dating until age 15 or 16?" She'd say no to a freshman going to the prom, even if the child gets mad. And McClintock would put limits on the movies and TV programs kids watch, especially younger kids. By the time they're in their late teens, you won't have as much control, but if they've had guidance when they were younger, they'll recognize destructive messages about sex.

She also suggests you make your house the center of activity, the place where kids congregate. Provide food and a place to watch videos, then stay home to supervise. "Your social life may have to go on the back burner for a while," McClintock says. "We're all busy and tired, but we have to be more available. There are a lot of lonely kids out there."

Working parents should be aware that a frequent site of sexual activity is at home after school. Not every parent can be home, but you can set up firm rules or even enlist another adult to supervise.

McClintock says she would also put limits on the clothing kids wear. Many current styles are sexually suggestive. No one is advocating a return to long petticoats and knee-length swim suits, but kids don't have to wear styles that openly display their bodies either. Let them know that a degree of modesty is okay.

Parents should get their kids involved in activities, McClintock suggests. Sports, drama, music, and art all fill time and give kids a healthy, constructive outlet. If your church doesn't have a youth group, get one started. It's important for kids to have a constructive place to go with their friends on Friday night.

Kids also need to know the fallacy of the "condom gospel" preached in the media. "Kids hear, 'We can protect you from pregnancy and disease, just use a condom and have safe sex.' Whatever that means," Dr. Schaeffer says. She points out that condoms can and do fail. Babies and STDs can and do result. Kids need to know that.

Providing kids with knowledge of, and access to, contraceptives is a thorny issue. There are those who say that easy access just gives kids permission to have sex. There are others who say that if kids decide to have sex, even though they know it's wrong, at least giving them contraceptives will prevent pregnancy.

"I think you have to know your child. If you have talked and talked and you realize the child still is or will soon be having sex, do you give him or her contraceptives? I do. But that's a physician's viewpoint—I don't want them to make two mistakes," Dr. Schaeffer says. "I know it's like saying, 'I don't want you to start a fire, but if you do, here's a fire extinguisher.' It's hard.

"One way to handle it is to talk with kids about contraception," Dr. Schaeffer adds. "But always say, 'These are the [things] we use in marriage to not have children until we are ready.' That puts it in the context of God's plan for us."

McClintock thinks if your child is dating someone it's okay to ask if he or she is thinking about having sex. If kids can talk to parents about their feelings, it may help them see why they should keep their sexual urges in check. And it opens the door for honest discussion.

In my own family, there was no topic relating to

sex or the human condition we did not talk about. Some members of the older generation would have been shocked at some of the discussions we had! My kids knew exactly what contraceptives were and how they work, but I don't think that gave them permission to have sex. There was never any doubt in their minds about our values.

We also treated sex with a sense of humor that kept it in proportion. I think it's healthy for kids to know that while sex is important, it's not the main focus of adult life. Again, that provides a balance to the media's message.

What if, despite your best efforts, your kids have sex? "It can happen in any family," says McClintock. "It doesn't mean you weren't a good parent."

She speaks from painful experience. Her daughter became pregnant as a teenager, the first time she had sex. She chose to keep the baby. "Her whole life has changed," she says. "She's going to college, but she doesn't date. She can't visit friends, go on spring break, do all the things her friends do. He's a beautiful little boy and the most important thing in her life, but the whole experience was very painful."

Faith in God's love and forgiveness is what got the family through. "We as Christians can go to the Lord and wrestle it out in front of Him, and He makes it okay," she says.

Further Reading
Reed, Bobbie. *Surviving Your Child's Dating Years: Seven Vital Skills that Help Your Child Build Healthy Relationships.* St. Louis: Concordia Publishing House, 1995.

The Learning About Sex Series (Discussion sheets with leaders notes are available for each title.)

Buth, Lenore. *How to Talk Confidently with Your Child About Sex: And Appreciate Your Own Sexuality Too.* St. Louis: Concordia Publishing House, 1995.

Greene, Carol. *Why Boys and Girls Are Different.* (Ages 3 to 5) St. Louis: Concordia Publishing House, 1995.

Hummel, Ruth. *Where Do Babies Come From?* (Ages 6 to 8) St. Louis: Concordia Publishing House, 1995.

Graver, Jane. *How You Are Changing.* (Ages 8 to 11) St. Louis: Concordia Publishing House, 1995.

Bimler, Richard. *Sex and the New You.* (Ages 11 to 14) St. Louis: Concordia Publishing House, 1995.

Ameiss, Bill, and Jane Graver. *Love, Sex and God.* (Ages 14 to 18) St. Louis: Concordia Publishing House, 1995.

6

Expose Abortion's Big Lie

At just 5′ 3″, Alice doesn't look like a basketball star. But in high school and college, basketball was her life. It was so important that she aborted her baby so she wouldn't be cut from the team. Listen while she tells her story.

"My dream was to play college basketball, but since I was so short, I didn't think I ever would. But there was a college that wanted *me!* I was really excited when I headed off to campus. Practice started right away, but I was going home every weekend to see my boyfriend from high school. We'd party and all that stuff.

"Within the first month of college, I was pregnant. It just put a wrench in my whole life. The coach hadn't even made the first cut yet, and I didn't know how I could possibly play basketball pregnant. And to me, basketball was my only hope for acceptance, for making something of my life.

"I told my boyfriend I wanted an abortion. He kind of knew my mind was set on it, but he didn't say no. I never told my dad or my sisters. My mother had died when I was 9 years old. My boyfriend picked me up at college, and we went to a clinic.

"I was pretty frightened. He waited in the lounge, and they took me into a small room with a table, like at a gynecologist's office. It was a suction abortion, and I vomited through the whole thing. I just could not stop throwing up. I don't know if it was the procedure itself, or what I was feeling.

"I don't think it quite clicked that this was a baby. To me it was just a problem. But maybe in the back of my mind, I knew it was, and I was sick about that.

"When it was over, they gave me some orange juice, but I couldn't drink it. I sat there for quite a while. Finally my boyfriend helped me to the car for the six-hour drive back to school. I was so out of it. I was just rolling around in the back seat, moaning.

"I was in bed for a week in intense pain and with heavy bleeding and a fever. My roommate was very worried about me. Of course I missed a whole week of practice, and I got cut from the team. I was totally devastated. I couldn't believe that after all I'd gone through the coach would cut me.

"I kept seeing my boyfriend for a few months, but then we just couldn't handle it anymore. You can't have a relationship with something like that hanging there. I honestly can't remember some of those days, the path I was taking was so destructive. I remember smoking pot while I was driving a car, just swerving all over the road and thinking it was really funny. I don't think I ever felt any guilt for the abortion—I just buried it very deep.

"Then I met another fellow—Steve—who is now my husband. I confided in him about the abortion, once I realized that he was someone I wanted to spend the rest of my life with. He was very understanding and kind about it. After my second year of college, I dropped out. Steve had graduated and had a job, and we got married.

"About that time my 15-year-old sister got pregnant. I think that's when it finally started to hit me, what I had done. I watched her go through her whole pregnancy and give up the baby for adoption, and it was very hard because I knew that I could have done that too.

"One night it all sort of came to a head. I just lost it. I went into a closet and I was pulling my hair out by the roots. I just completely lost control.

"After I calmed down a little, I called my older sister, even though it was two o'clock in the morning. She was a Christian. Somehow I knew she was different, and I knew I could go to her with this and she'd have the answers I needed. I was sobbing over the phone so hard she told me to come over. I went, and I just poured my guts out. I told her and her husband the whole story.

"After about two hours of confession and crying, they sat down with me with a book that goes over the whole salvation process. I was just amazed. I'd never heard it before. God was really working in me because it all became so clear to me then. I prayed for a long time with them. It really was a miracle.

"Things have been so different since that day. God has really worked in my life. I have three healthy children now, and my husband also became a strong Christian. It's just neat."

Alice's story isn't unique. Many young girls who get pregnant unintentionally are persuaded by abortion's big lie: "It's just a clump of cells ... Abortion is no worse than having a tooth pulled ... Take charge, make a positive decision, and get on with your life." Too many of them find later—and for some the realization comes years later—that they bitterly regret listening to abortion's siren song.

Women who have deep doubts but have an abortion anyway to "solve a problem" are at risk for a wide range of psychological problems, none of them pleasant.

- **Guilt.** A young woman who later realizes that it was her baby she aborted can be overwhelmed with guilt. It can color her whole view of herself and lead to self-hatred and punishment.
- **Anxiety.** Tension, pounding heart, frequent headaches, insomnia, generalized worry, and difficulty concentrating can lead a woman to quit school or withdraw from life.
- **Emotional numbness.** A young woman may try to flatten her emotions so she won't feel anything too deeply. It can be hard for her to commit herself in future relationships.
- **Depression.** Many women suffer a constant low-level sadness. A few actually become clinically depressed.
- **Distressing psychological responses.** Some women experience stress on the anniversary of the abortion or the baby's due date. Others experience flashbacks when they have a gynecological exam or hear the hum of machinery that sounds like the abortion equipment. Some have dreams in which babies are lost or crying.
- **Destructive behavior.** Some young women use

alcohol or drugs to numb the pain. Others become sexually promiscuous or enter abusive relationships. While no one can say that abortion is the reason for such self-destructive behavior, studies have reported a higher incidence in women who have had an abortion.[1]

- **Increased risk of breast cancer.** A recent study by Janet Daling of the Fred Hutchinson Cancer Research Center in Seattle, Washington, shows that women who abort a first pregnancy increase their risk of breast cancer by 50 percent on average. If the woman is under the age of 18, her risk rises by 800 percent. The media has not trumpeted this information in the way they have other cancer risks.[2]

What Do Women Who Have Abortions Have in Common?

I have interviewed many women who have had abortions, some who had an abortion recently and others whose abortions happened many years ago. In asking them to recall what their childhoods were like, several patterns emerge.

- **Distance in the family.** While there were certainly exceptions, the majority of the women I talked to came from families that were emotionally cool. Sadly, many of them said that they were never sure their parents loved them. "I suppose they did, but they never said it," was a common theme. A few families were actually dysfunctional, including physical and emotional abuse.
- **Silence in the family about sex.** Many of the women said, "We just didn't talk about THAT!" When kids

grow up thinking sex is something furtive and slightly dirty and then find out in their teens that it's not, they are more at risk to experiment.

- **A feeling of not being able to talk to parents.** Several women said they didn't want to tell their parents they were pregnant for fear of being thrown out. Others were afraid to tell for fear of disappointing their parents. The irony is that almost all the parents, when they found out after the fact, said, "Why didn't you come to us? We would have helped. You didn't have to have an abortion." At the time, the women didn't feel that support.

- **A lack of support from the baby's father.** I don't mean to bash men, but most of the young men involved, probably because of their own immaturity, abandoned the women either before the abortion or shortly after. Women who are pregnant out of wedlock generally face it alone.

- **A feeling of having no choice.** "I didn't really want an abortion, but I had no choice." I heard these words over and over. Alone, deserted by boyfriend and parents, without money, and often without job skills, the women saw only one friend willing to help—the abortion clinic.

While taking a course in methods of statistical research at Marquette University, I did a mini-research study in which I sent questionnaires about family background to a group of women who had become pregnant outside of marriage. Based on a theory called Family Communication Patterns, their answers placed them into one of four types of families:

- **Pluralistic.** These families stress thinking and discussing issues on an intellectual level. Children aren't prevented from expressing their opinions even if they differ from those of their parents.
- **Protective.** These families stress obedience and conformity and discourage conflict.
- **Laissez-faire.** There doesn't seem to be much communication in these families. There are few expectations, and the children raise themselves.
- **Consensual.** These families try to balance two opposing forces: the need for thinking for oneself and the need for harmony and conformity. Parents encourage self-expression on the part of their children but draw the line at conflict.

According to my small study, of the women who had chosen abortion, the greatest percentage came from protective families, which stress obedience and unquestioning acceptance of authority. Those women who came from consensual families, which balanced authority and thinking for oneself, had the lowest abortion rate.

While my study was too small to be statistically significant (so the results can't be applied to the general population), the professor remarked that the general trend was strong and indicated "something is happening here."

Which style does your family fall into? You may want to talk to your pastor or a counselor if you feel you need help in being more open with your children.

What Can Parents Do?

In the chapter about sexual promiscuity, we discussed ways to prevent your children from becoming sexually active before marriage. Remember, kids need effective sex education. Silence about sex *does not* keep teens from learning about it. They just learn in all the wrong places. In addition, you need to help your kids see through the big lie of "abortion as the solution."

- **Establish an approachable climate in your home from early childhood on.** Can your child talk to you? Have you made it clear that there are no "unspeakable topics" in your home? Your daughter has to know that even if you disapprove of what she has done, you will always love and support her. She needs to know that nothing she could do would ever cause you to "throw her out." She has to hear you *say* that. She needs to know she has other solutions—finding that out after an abortion is tragic. God, because of Jesus, loves your child unconditionally. Remind your child that God comes to her—in His Word, in Baptism, in His Holy Supper—to love and guide her through every situation, no matter how desperate.

- **Talk with your kids, as part of their sex education, about the abortion process.** Kids need to know that what is referred to as a "blob of tissue" or a "clump of cells" is a human life. Your daughter needs to know that while the first reaction of women who have abortions is usually relief, psychological distress often comes later. Information from France, where RU 486 (the "abortion pill") is used, shows an even greater risk of psychological aftermath as a result of that method. The woman sees the fetus she expels rather than having it sucked into an opaque container.[3] Your child should know about the increased risk of breast cancer in women who have abortions.

- **Tell your kids that the fathers of aborted babies can also suffer psychological distress.** Even though their initial response is also likely to be relief, men aren't exempt from the destructive effects of abortion. One man, the father of a baby aborted years before, told me that it has "haunted" him all his life. Your son needs to know that.
- **Both sons and daughters need to know that there are alternatives.** Several million infertile couples in this country would give anything to give a baby a home.

If the unthinkable happens and your teenage daughter—or your son's girlfriend—becomes pregnant, you must be sure they know that abortion is not the easy answer it would seem to be. Tell your child you will support her in either keeping the baby or placing it for adoption. Remind your child that through Baptism, the baby becomes God's specially chosen child, an heir to eternal life.

If, God forbid, you find out that your daughter has had an abortion, you have a double burden. You need to grieve for the grandchild you have lost, but you also have to help your daughter deal with her emotions, even though they may be deeply buried.

Most of all your daughter needs to hear the message of God's love and forgiveness. She needs to know that He can forgive any sin, even this one. Don't try to deal with this yourself. Your best friend in this case may be a loving, caring minister who can bring God's message of comfort and healing. There are some women who need professional help to cope with the aftermath of abortion. A Christian therapist can be invaluable.

Don't discount the need to help a son cope if his girlfriend has an abortion. He needs to confront his feelings and hear the message of God's love and forgiveness as much as the young woman does.

The world is still selling the lie of abortion: It's easy, painless, and the best choice. Kids need to know the truth. And they need to know that God can bring healing, even into the destruction of abortion's aftermath.

"There are still days when I cry on Steve's shoulder," Alice says. "But it's because of who I did that to, who could be sitting here with me today. It isn't because I feel guilty about it anymore. God has really healed me of that. I still feel bad about it. I'll obviously never be happy about it. But I don't feel like I need to go on punishing myself about it because God has forgiven me and I can forgive myself."

Further Reading
Reardon, David C. *Aborted Women, Silent No More*. Gaithersburg, Maryland: Human Life International, 1987.

Reisser, Teri. *Help for the Post-Abortion Woman*. Grand Rapids: Zondervan, 1989.

Winkler, Kathleen. *When the Crying Stops: Abortion, the Pain and the Healing*. Milwaukee: Northwestern Publishing House, 1992.

Notes
1. Teri Reisser, *Help for the Post-Abortion Woman*, (Grand Rapids: Zondervan, 1989).
2. Christine Gorman, "Do Abortions Raise the Risk of Breast Cancer?" *Time* (November 7, 1994): 61.
3. Louise Levathes, "Listening to RU 486," *Health* (January/February 1995): 86–90.

7
Deflate the High of Alcohol and Drugs

One fall Friday night during my son's senior year in college, he found a young woman in the jeans-and-leather-jacket college uniform staggering around his car. She was peering up at the number of the house where he lived. When Brad asked if he could help, she slurred through an incoherent story about trying to find a party somewhere in the area. Realizing she was dangerously drunk, he offered to drive her to the party. She gratefully collapsed into his car, and they set out on a futile hunt for the address she'd been given. There was no such number. He offered to drive her home. He was shocked to learn she lived in the freshman dorm. She'd only been at college a few weeks.

Arriving at the dorm, he escorted her up to her room to be sure she got there safely. But he couldn't let her go in without a warning. He told her how lucky she was that the person who had picked her up was not someone who would take advantage of her. He told her the next time she might not be so lucky. And he tried to put the fear of God into her about the dangers of drinking.

Brad never saw that girl again. But the story has stuck in my mind, not only because I'm proud of my son's actions—I am—but because I feared for that young woman. I would guess it was not her first experience with alcohol nor her last. She probably wasn't more than 18, and she was playing Russian roulette with something that could permanently change her life in an instant. Or end it.

Alcohol and other drug use is epidemic among America's young people. And not just at colleges. It starts younger. Much younger. Surveys by the National Institute on Drug Abuse, the National Council on Alcoholism, and the University of Michigan have unearthed some frightening statistics:

- Average age for first alcohol use in the United States is 12, for drugs, 13.
- More than half of high school seniors have tried an illegal drug.
- Seventy percent of eighth-graders have tried alcohol. More than a third of high school seniors say their friends get drunk at least once a week.
- A survey done by *Weekly Reader* said a third of fourth-graders were feeling peer pressure to try alcohol. Fourth-graders![1]

It's a drug-saturated world our children are entering. Some parents take comfort in the fact that they don't live in the inner-city. "Kids out here in the suburbs don't do that stuff," they think.

Wrong, says police officer Denis Dutton, a Drug Abuse Resistance Education (D.A.R.E.) instructor who leads the program in Christian grade schools in suburban Milwaukee. "It's not true that drugs and alcohol are inner-city problems," Dutton says. "Certainly those areas have risk factors, but there are drinking and drug problems in suburbs and rural areas too. No matter where you live, every youngster goes through all the stages of growing up and faces a tremendous amount of peer pressure and temptation."

Who uses alcohol and drugs? Angry kids. Rebellious kids. Nice kids. The kids next door. No kids, including your own, are immune. What's a parent to do? The problem can seem so enormous that it's tempting to retreat, to shut out the facts and just say, "Not my kids. They wouldn't do that."

That's a naive response. Anyone's kids can make a mistake. Anyone's kids can get caught up in an experiment. And when you are dealing with something as dangerous as alcohol or drugs, a mistake can blight, or even end, a young life.

Dutton points out some characteristics in kids that put them at increased risk for alcohol and drug abuse.

- Low self-esteem. "It's the number 1 factor because kids who don't like themselves are easy prey for anything that will make them feel better," Dutton says.
- Isolation, feelings of alienation from family and friends, and difficulty accepting authority.
- A broken or dysfunctional family, especially if there is no father in the home.
- School problems. Poor performance, low grades, and feeling overwhelmed by academic pressure can lead to drug and alcohol use.

- Difficulty expressing thoughts and feelings or poor communication skills.
- Inability to cope with stress and frustration.
- Feelings of anxiety, depression, or boredom.
- Little self-discipline or lack of personal achievement.
- A great need for acceptance coupled with the inability to resist peer pressure. All kids want to be accepted by the group—that's part of being a kid. But when a child's need for acceptance is overwhelming, he or she may do anything to be part of the group.
- A desire to feel older, more independent, or "cool."
- An unassertive personality, which can result in being afraid to say no to anyone.
- A need to escape uncomfortable feelings or to feel good.
- A belief that "everybody does it." It may be too late before the child realizes that everybody is not doing it and he's in the wrong group.

Families at high risk for their kids to abuse alcohol and drugs also share some characteristics.
- Parents who don't show affection for their children.
- Parents who neglect or abuse their children.
- Parents who either are too lenient or too strict.
- Parents or others in the family who abuse alcohol or use drugs.

- A family with no rules or rules that are not clearly defined or enforced.
- Parents who do not discuss or discourage alcohol or drug use.
- Families with little communication among family members.[2]

One group of high school students in California was surveyed on why they use drugs or alcohol. The students listed five primary reasons: to get away from problems, to experiment, because their friends use, because it makes them feel good, and because they have nothing else to do.[3]

Drinking and drug use among teens usually develops in four stages, says Dr. David Elkind, a professor of child study at Tufts University.

In the first stage, Dr. Elkind says, the young person tries out the substance and likes how it makes him or her feel. During the next stage, the teen starts to look for opportunities to drink or use. There are some noticeable changes in behavior—new friends, loss of concern about appearance or schoolwork, unusual irritability, or passivity. At the third stage, the teen is becoming alcohol or drug dependent, and getting high becomes the top priority. He or she may skip school, steal to get money for alcohol or drugs, and show distinct changes in eating and sleeping patterns. At the fourth, or addicted, stage, the young person *needs* alcohol or drugs just to feel normal.[4]

Preventing a child from ever entering this destructive cycle is the best thing a parent can do. The only way to do that, says Dutton, is through education. "I hear parents say, 'My kids don't need to know about that stuff,' but I disagree," he says. "Kids' naivete can be destructive when they don't know what they're dealing with. Not having information is detrimental."

Preparing your kids to deal with the world of alcohol and drugs puts a burden on you, the parent. You have to educate yourself first before you can educate your children. Just saying "Stay away from that stuff" won't do it. Giving kids inaccurate information is worse than giving them no information. They won't take you seriously if they know what you are saying isn't true. So arm yourself with accurate information.

Where do you find correct information? Start with your public library. Your local police department probably has information on drugs. You can get reams of information from the U. S. government (see the resource list at the end of this chapter).

Overview of Common Drugs

One brief chapter can't cover all available drugs nor can it give complete information on each one. But here's a quick rundown of the most common.

Alcohol

Beer, wine, and wine coolers are teen favorites. Alcohol is a depressant, which slows brain and central nervous system functions. Drinking causes impaired judgment and coordination, emotional instability, and aggression. It's a factor in a high percentage of teen deaths from car crashes, other accidents, and acute alcohol poisoning. It's often linked with sexual experimentation that can result in pregnancy or sexually transmitted diseases. Drinking is also a factor in date rape.

Marijuana

This drug is most often smoked, but sometimes it's eaten in food. Paraphernalia for marijuana use includes cigarette papers, clips for holding the cigarette (called a joint or roach), pipes, or water pipes. Marijuana is a central nervous system depressant that causes hallucinations. Some people get panic reactions when using it. Long-term health effects include impaired memory, extreme lethargy, and decreased sexual function. Marijuana also may cause lung cancer. Symptoms of use include intoxication; impairment of judgment, memory, and coordination; fatigue; and red eyes.

Inhalants

This group of drugs is especially popular among teens because they are cheap, legal, and give a quick high. Kids sniff solvents, glue, gasoline, lighter fluid, typewriter correction fluid, and just about any type of aerosol. The substances are usually sprayed into a plastic bag and inhaled. They depress the central nervous system and produce a feeling of intoxication along with dream-like sensations or hallucinations that last from 15 minutes to several hours. Brain damage is a big risk along with lung, liver, and kidney damage. Kids also can burn out the respiratory passages. Kids have died from heart failure or suffocation while sniffing.

Cocaine

Cocaine looks like powdered sugar and can be sniffed or smoked. Crack, a paste-like form of concentrated cocaine that's hardened into small rock-like balls, is one of the most addictive substances on the street. Cheap and easily available, crack can hook a person in just a few uses. Cocaine stimulates the central nervous system and increases breathing and heart rate. This drug can cause heart attacks and strokes in otherwise healthy young people. Symptoms of use include dilated pupils, loss of appetite, agitation, paranoia, and an inability to sleep.[5]

There are many more drugs available, including hallucinogens such as LSD, tranquilizers, sedatives, and narcotics. All of these are sometimes used by kids. Learn about them.

You also need to know the most common places kids use alcohol and drugs. It may surprise you to learn that the most common spot is in a child's home, especially after school when parents are not yet home, or in the child's bedroom behind closed doors. Other common places are:

- at friends' homes, especially during parties;
- in the car;
- on a date; or
- outdoors, at the beach or a park.[6]

Prevention

Now that you know a bit more about why and

how kids use alcohol and drugs, you have to deal with the big question—what can you do to prevent your child from becoming involved? First, be aware that some ways of approaching kids don't work very well.

- **Denial.** Pretending there's no problem, that drug and alcohol use doesn't exist in your child's school or among his or her friends, won't make it go away. It will just stop you from taking action.

- **Overreaction.** Finding out your child has tried a few sips of beer and grounding him for a year or sending him to a drug assessment program might be going after a fly with a cannon. Obviously you should never ignore any alcohol or drug use, but don't make your child a criminal for one small slip.

- **Threatening.** "If I ever find out you are using drugs, I'll throw you out in the street" or "Your father will kill you" won't stop a kid from experimenting. Threats will just weaken your communication.

- **Scare tactics.** Kids will see right through it if you tell them they will die the first time they touch alcohol! Teach your children the very real dangers but base your warnings on fact.

- **Bribery.** You can't bribe your kids to avoid alcohol or drugs. "I'll buy you a car if you never drink" just invites the child to manipulate you.

- **Drinking at home.** Allowing your kids to drink in your house so they won't do it elsewhere only tells them you think teenage drinking is okay. It may also bring legal trouble.

- **Guilt.** "If you love me, you won't drink" probably won't produce anything but anger!
- **Rescuing.** Protecting kids from the consequences of their actions will only encourage the same behavior. Paying their fines, getting a lawyer to get them off the hook, bailing them out of trouble are all examples of "enabling" in social work jargon.[7]

If those tactics don't work, what does? Open communication and solid information, combined with a zero tolerance for alcohol and drug use, says Dutton. He offers some suggestions.

- **Encourage open communication in your family.** Start at a young age. Talk with your kids about everything. Don't have any closed subjects in your home.
- **Tell your kids you love them, that they are special gifts of God.** Build their self-esteem through appropriate praise. Spend time with them. Do things together. Celebrate often the new life that Christ won for them on the cross.
- **Get your kids involved in extracurricular activities, especially at church and school.** Busy kids won't drift into drinking or drug use because of boredom.
- **Sit your teens down and talk about alcohol and drugs.** Share the information you've learned in a straightforward way. Make sure they know the dangers and possible consequences of drinking and using drugs. Emphasize God's gift of healthy

bodies and the responsibility we have toward Him for their maintenance.

- **Make it clear that your policy is no alcohol or drug use.** You can't waffle on this one. The policy is NONE. Tell your kids why and point out that God has placed you in authority to help them grow up safely.
- **If you have an occasional drink yourself, make sure your kids know that in your family you use alcohol legally and responsibly.** Using alcohol legally means when you are over 21. Using it responsibly means not to excess and never when driving.
- **Know your kids' friends and, if possible, their parents.** Some parents have banded together to agree that any party at their homes will be supervised and alcohol-free. Always know where your kids are going. Don't be afraid to call other parents to find out if a party will be supervised.
- **Set up a code word with your kids that they can use if they're in a bad situation.** Agree that if they use the word in a phone call, you'll come and get them immediately, no questions asked.
- **Make your home inviting so it becomes the social center for your kids and their friends.** Be there—not in the same room but still in the house and available. Then you are in charge. Never allow any alcohol use at your home. Not only does looking the other way undermine your message, but if a child is picked up by the authorities and under the

influence of alcohol he or she got at your house, you could go to jail.

- **Have consequences for what your kids do.** If they do experiment with drinking or drugs, make the consequences swift and sure. Taking away a car, grounding a teen, making him or her pay for any damages, or assigning some menial chores are all things parents have used successfully.

- **Be sure your kids know the legal consequences of their actions.** A drunk driving conviction can bring jail time. Drug possession surely will.

- **Visiting a drug rehab center or the scene of a drunk driving accident might be drastic but worthwhile.** Watching newscasts about accidents, television movies about alcoholism or drug addiction, and reading newspaper stories about the consequences of drinking or taking drugs can make a big impression. A family in our town was sued by the parents of a child who died from alcohol he got in their home. The family lost everything. I remember my brother sitting his school-age kids down and reading them the story from the paper. That can make kids think about what they do.

- **Encourage your children's school to offer a drug education program.** There are many available, including the D.A.R.E. program (taught by police officers). Make sure, though, that your school's program tells children clearly that alcohol and drug use is wrong. A few programs concentrate on giving children decision-making skills and allowing them to decide for themselves what is right for them. Most young children aren't capable of making those kinds of moral decisions. They need to be told DON'T DO IT.

What if, despite all your efforts at education, your kids do abuse alcohol or drugs? First, you have to know the signs so you will realize what's happening. Here are some things to watch for in your own child.

- Does he act intoxicated? Does she stagger, slur words, throw up, or pass out?
- Have you smelled alcohol on his breath or a "burnt rope" odor clinging to her clothes?
- Has your child's sleeping pattern changed? Is he suffering from insomnia, oversleeping, or sleeping at inappropriate times?
- Has your child lost weight or experienced a loss of appetite?
- Is she neglecting her personal appearance or grooming?
- Have you noticed behavioral changes such as moodiness, depression, anxiety, irritability, hypersensitivity, hostility, or lethargy?
- Has your child lost interest in former activities?
- Have you observed a change in the friends with whom your child associates or an unwillingness to introduce new friends?
- Have your child's values, ideals, and beliefs changed?
- Are your child's grades slipping? Is she exhibiting

a loss of interest in schoolwork or talking about dropping out of school? Is he sleeping in class?
- Is there any unusual behavior problems at school?
- Have you seen changes in your child's room? Is his door always closed? Is there a scent of incense or room deodorizers? Have you found drug paraphernalia such as unfamiliar small containers, plastic bags, or locked boxes?
- Is your child using eye drops, mouthwash, or breath mints more frequently?
- Is money or valuables missing from the house?

If your child has an alcohol or drug problem, he or she needs professional help. This is not something a parent can handle. Call a hospital with a drug and alcohol abuse program for information. Try to find one that specializes in dealing with teenage abusers.

If your child comes home highly intoxicated, it's a medical emergency. More than one teen has been put to bed to "sleep it off" and found dead in the morning. Take your child to an emergency room.

Did the girl my son helped ever learn her lesson? Did her family and friends let her know how destructive her behavior was? We'll never know. But I do know that if you don't teach your kids what's wrong with drinking and using drugs, you are leaving them open to learn by trial and error. In this case, one error can mean a life changed forever or even lost.

Don't wait until your child is ready to head off to college. By then it's much too late. "Education has to be ongoing, it can't be done just once," Dutton says. "And it's never too early to start."

Further Reading

Barun, Ken, and Philip Bashe. *How to Keep the Children You Love Off Drugs.* New York: Atlantic Monthly Press, 1988.

Perkins, William M., and Nancy McMurtrie-Perkins. *Raising Drug-Free Kids in a Drug-Filled World.* San Francisco: Hazelden, 1986.

Wilmes, David J. *Parenting for Prevention: How to Raise a Child to Say No to Alcohol/Drugs.* Minneapolis: Johnson Institute Books, 1989.

U. S. Department of Education. *Growing Up Drug Free: A Parent's Guide to Prevention.* This publication includes an extensive bibliography and list of sources to contact for help. To order, call 1-800-624-0100. Or write to Growing Up Drug Free, Pueblo, CO 81009.

Notes

1. Statistics from Ken Barun and Philip Bashe, *How to Keep the Children You Love Off Drugs,* (New York: Atlantic Monthly Press, 1988) and Joel Blaylock, "Keeping Your Jr. Highers Drug Free," *Jr. High Ministry* (October/November 1992).
2. Barun and Bashe, 68.
3. Ibid, 47.
4. David Elkind, "Teens and Alcohol," *Parents* (January 1991).
5. David J. Wilmes, *Parenting for Prevention: How to Raise a Child to Say No to Alcohol/Drugs,* (Minneapolis: Johnson Institute Books, 1989): 24–30.
6. Ibid, 33.
7. William M. Perkins, and Nancy McMurtrie-Perkins, *Raising Drug-Free Kids in a Drug-Filled World,* (San Francisco: Hazelden, 1986): 17–21.

8

Deglamorize Gangs, Guns, and Violence

The historic church looms large on its inner-city corner. Its gothic arches soar, its steeple towers, its stained-glass windows glow like jewels in the morning sun. Once a large and prosperous parish, it now struggles in a changing world. The streets it overlooks, quiet and peaceful on Sunday mornings, can be mean and dangerous at other hours.

After services a small group of parents huddles around a table in the church office, reflecting on their lives as inner-city parents. They share their fears for their children and their efforts to protect them from the values and the violence of the streets on which they live.

"I'm trying to keep my kids from growing up the way I grew up," says Devonne, an earnest young African-American man about to become stepfather to two small children. "I was in a gang, was about 13 when I first got involved. I was looking for easy money. And I had nobody else to turn to. There was nobody to listen to me. They listened."

While this group of parents faces the extra challenge of raising kids in an inner-city environment, let's be very clear about one thing: Gangs, guns, and violence know no race and no socioeconomic class. While kids involved in violence may be statistically more common in America's crumbling inner cities, police in suburban and rural areas report a frightening escalation of gang warfare. And while gangs used to be a primarily male phenomenon, growing numbers of girls are becoming involved, either in gangs of their own or as members of an "auxiliary" to a male gang.

Why? Because of the breakdown of families, says police officer Leon Staples of the Community Service Division of the Milwaukee Police Department.

Why Kids Join Gangs

Staples, who was a gang crime officer for 12 years, is a tough, down-to-the-nitty-gritty African-American policeman who has seen gang warfare from the inside. He's lived and raised a family in the inner city. He doesn't hide what he's seen behind a screen of fancy words.

"Families used to be stronger," Staples says. "When parents said, 'You ain't gonna do that ... you gonna straighten up,' there was a better chance of a kid going right. Now you have what we call the dysfunctional family—one where anything is permitted, no discipline, no morals or values being taught, and especially no religion."

A large percentage of gang members come from families in which they have been physically or sexually abused or in which there is a history of violent behavior, Staples says. Many gang members' families are filled with drug and alcohol abuse. Children of parents who are unemployed, who dropped out of school, or who had children while they were still in their teens are more at risk to become involved in gangs and violence.

There are other factors besides the breakdown of families that have led to the explosion of gangs and violence, according to Staples. These include:

- **The glamorization of gangs in the media.** "Kids see it on TV and in the newspapers," Staples says. "Or they have a friend who is a gang member and they become a 'wanna be.' It's called peer pressure."

- **The easy money available from selling drugs.** Surprisingly, Staples says, most gang members don't use drugs harder than marijuana themselves. "Usually drug use is forbidden because they know drugs are habit-forming. Gang members are beaten or even executed if they use," he says. Instead the gangs form tight, well-organized "businesses" to sell drugs to others. Older gang members recruit young kids, often as young as age 9 or 10, into the business.

- **Our society's inflated desire for material things.** "Everybody wants to keep up with the Joneses, and kids dictate to parents what they are going to wear," Staples says. "You have to buy the kid $150 tennis shoes. When my son asked for them I said, 'Until K Mart and Target start selling them, you'll never have a pair!' " Staples also pointed out to his son that having those shoes would not make him into who he wanted to be. Realistically, just wearing the shoes could put him at risk to be robbed or even killed.

- **The normal adolescent desire for peer approval and acceptance.** Dr. Deborah Prothrow-Stith, assistant dean at the Harvard School of Public Health and author of *Deadly Consequences: How Violence Is Destroying Our Teenage Population,* says that hunger for approval has been perverted in gang life. All adolescent groups satisfy the same needs. "They provide young people with goals and objectives, a world view and a place where they are valued. Group membership gives some purpose to life."[1] Gang membership, she says, gives kids a feeling of recognition, of being noticed, of being special. Like all kids, gang members prefer negative attention to no attention at all. Devonne agrees. "I just wanted to be looked up to," he says.

- **Gangs give young males a feeling of what it means to be a man.** Gangs define a man as someone who is loyal to his friends and ruthless to his enemies, according to Dr. Prothrow-Stith. "These simple ideas make manhood accessible to many young men who cannot live up to the mainstream definition ... the capacity to make money," she writes.[2] In the gang, you don't have to have a job to be able to support your family or to feel like a man. You only need to be able to fight.

- **Young people's normal feelings of immortality.** Often teens don't grasp the permanence of dying, Dr. Prothrow-Stith says. They don't realize that bullet wounds *hurt.* They don't grasp the concept of a lifetime in a wheelchair from a gun injury. Teenagers, especially teen males, have always needed to show off a bit. They've always fought to determine their status in the pecking order. Minor clashes that used to be settled with fistfights too often today are settled with a gun.

The parents around the table in the church office don't have to be told about the dangers of the street. They know them well. They live with them every day.

"I worry about my daughter," says Laurie, a white single mother. "Somebody was shot and killed three blocks from her school while she was out on the playground. It bothers me that I can't be with her all the time."

"There are so many things out there that children are fascinated by," says Janelle, who is mother of a 3- and a 5-year-old and engaged to Devonne. "They see fast money, they see clout, they see an image. They don't see the negativity involved in getting there."

Prevention, the Best Answer

What can parents do to prevent their children from being caught up in the values of the street, from joining a gang with the violence it so often promotes? The following suggestions come from Leon Staples, Dr. Deborah Prothrow-Stith, and parents Devonne, Janelle, and Laurie.

- **Be in control.** "Have good discipline," says Staples. "Many parents break down under pressure. Let the kid do what he wants and he's on his way."
- **Educate your children about gangs and violence.** "I don't try to shield my kids from what's going on in the streets. I think that will just make them curious," says Janelle. "I teach them what's going on

out there and that it's not good for them."

"Sit kids down and tell them there's nothing in a gang that will help them," says Staples. "I tell them that I've seen kids get shot and the gang didn't do one thing to help them. They don't care.

"Educating your kids also means educating yourself," Staples adds. "You have to take time to learn about the signs and symbols gang members flash to each other, scrawl on walls and schoolbooks, or wear in jewelry. [Learn] the way they communicate through the colors of their clothes or the tilt of their baseball caps. Make sure your kids understand (you may be surprised to find they know more than you!) so they don't accidentally send a message they don't realize they're sending."

- **Foster an atmosphere of warmth and love in your home.** Build your children's self-esteem through acceptance and praise for what they do well. Remind your children often that Jesus loves them—enough to die for them. "Don't tear him down—that will turn him to the streets," Staples warns. Let your children hear you thanking God for them when you pray.

  "A lot of parents today are just disowning their children," adds Devonne, who has seen that happen in gang members' families. "When kids know they can't come back to their homes, who else are they going to go to? It's going to be the gang."

- **Communicate with your children.** That especially means listening. Remember Devonne's words—

They listened to me. "Make your children feel a part of the family," adds Laurie. "It's important they know they can come to you. If they can't or if you are too busy, they will find someone else."

- **Teach your children how to say no.** Let them know that drugs and alcohol will kill them and teach them how to resist, Staples says. That may mean giving your kids practice at saying no and planning with them how to escape a dangerous situation. Code words in a phone call can bring a parent fast!

- **Encourage your child's school to offer a D.A.R.E. program and a GREAT program (Gang Resistance Education and Training).** Both programs are offered through local police departments. Some schools also are offering conflict resolution programs in which trained peer mediators intervene in conflicts before fighting starts. Such a program teaches kids better ways to resolve differences.

- **If your kids are exposed to trauma—if they see street violence or it happens to someone they know—get them to talk about it.** They may talk to you, or take them to a counselor, but don't let it fester inside. "When children are exposed to violence, they run the risk of becoming overwhelmed," says Yale social worker Steven Nagler in an article on violence prevention in *Newsweek*.[3]

- **De-emphasize material things.** Explain to your children that things don't make the person. "I'm trying to teach my son already at the age of 5 not to buy the most expensive thing," says Janelle.

"I'm teaching him that he doesn't have to dress like everybody else, that he can be an individual and wear what he likes." She and Devonne agree that there are certain items they won't let their children wear when they are older, including the team jackets that gangs favor, certain styles of tennis shoes, and other gang fashions. "I don't want them robbed," Janelle says simply.

- **Emphasize education.** "Most gang members are functionally illiterate," Staples says. "Some of them are pretty smart, but they haven't stayed in school long enough to learn anything. They went to school on the streets." If your child has trouble in school, get help early. Dr. Prothrow-Stith says research shows that a high percentage of gang members have learning disabilities or other academic problems.

- **Be involved in family activities.** "Do things with your kids. Take them places—to museums or sports events," says Staples. "Let them know there are other things to do in life besides sit around and drink alcohol."

- **Always know who your children look up to as role models.** "The people on TV or in the news aren't good role models because they are usually doing something negative," says Janelle. Provide positive models through family, church, and school.

- **A father's role is critical.** "It's destructive when the father isn't part of the family," Devonne says. "Lots of men don't take time to be with their children." Devonne's own father lived across town from him and was not involved in his life.

- **Teach children that they can make a positive difference in the world.** "That's how my mother raised me. That's how I'm raising my children" says Janelle. "I'm a black woman, part of the black community, raised in the so-called ghetto, but I've been able to make a difference." She tries to model that attitude to her children.

- **If you are struggling with low income yourself, resist the quick infusion of cash that can come from kids involved in drug sales.** Dr. Prothrow-Stith speaks of parents who look the other way when kids give them money. Staples mentions parents who don't ask questions when a child comes home with an expensive new coat or shoes. "When I was growing up, if I came home with a coat and said a friend gave it to me, my mother would take me and the coat and find out where it came from," he says. "Parents aren't doing that today."

- **Control where your kids go.** Staples says his daughter used to ask to go to a skating rink notorious for gang fights at night. "I'd say, 'Sure, but you're going on Saturday morning and I'm going with you.' Somehow on Saturday morning she'd have lost interest!" he chuckles. Children should not dictate to their parents where they are going and when, Staples emphasizes.

- **Most important, center your family's life in God.** "Teach your children to love God first. Tell them 'With God in your heart, you can do anything,' "

Janelle says. It was meeting Janelle and seeing her strong faith that helped draw Devonne out of the gang. He now works as a teacher's aide in their church school. "God played a big part," he says. "He made it easier to get out." Children who grow up secure in the knowledge that they are loved by Christ don't need to look elsewhere for love and security. Make worship a priority in your family and apply what you learn and taste of God's grace each week to the struggles your child faces.

Warning Signs

How do you know if your child is flirting with joining a gang? There are some clues to watch for, Staples says.

- **Gang signs and symbols in your kid's room or on his belongings.** Pitchforks, five- or six-pointed stars, crowns, or combinations of letters and numbers are all suspect.
- **Gang clothing.** Look for baseball caps worn with a distinctive tilt to the right or left, certain team jackets, or certain color combinations (especially blue and black, red and black, or gold and black) that the child wants to wear all the time. You can get information on gang colors and styles in your area from your local police department.
- **References to your child's friends as "my people" or "my folks."** Each phrase denotes a different gang.
- **New friends, especially if they are significantly**

older than your child. Normal 18- or 19-year-olds don't want to hang around with 12- or 13-year-olds.

- **Tatoos.** Tatooed gang symbols generally mean the child is a hardcore gang member. "Seek help right away, before he becomes involved in criminal activity," says Staples.
- **Jewelry with gang symbols in the design.** Some jewelry companies deliberately manufacture gold jewelry with gang symbols because they know it sells. "They don't care about life, they care about making money," says Staples.
- **Truancy or poor progress in school.** If your child talks about dropping out, you should be worried. Too often dropping out of school means dropping into a gang.
- **Money from unexplained sources or new, expensive items you know your child can't afford.** The money has to come from somewhere. Too often it's coming from drug sales.

Finding Help

If you see signs of gang involvement in your child's behavior, what do you do? "Get help," says Staples. "You can't handle this yourself."

Turn first to your police department. They may have social workers trained in working with kids who are at risk or are in a gang. Or call a social service agency that specializes in working with at-risk kids. Sometimes they offer what are called diversion programs. Your local United Way office may be able to help you locate one.

You also may find help from your church. While the prayers and support of your pastor will certainly help, some ministers don't know how to deal with problems of gang membership and violence. It may take a counselor with specialized training to get through to at-risk kids.

Once the child decides to leave the gang, the problem may become worse. Gangs don't give up their members easily. "It was hard getting out," Devonne says. "When I left, everyone said things like, 'Oh, you think you're too good for us now!' I kept telling them, 'I've got my own life now. I have things to value. I have to do what I have to do to make it.'"

Devonne was fortunate because he had enough authority within the gang that members didn't threaten him physically when he left. Other members who try to leave may not fare so well. A child coming out of a gang may need extra family support as well as counseling.

"Gangs emphasize love and loyalty," Staples says, "but those are lies because true love and loyalty don't exist in a gang." Kids have to see that real love and loyalty come from God and family, not a gang. Then they will be able to resist the allure of gangs.

"Parents who think they can put blinders on and this is going to go away need to know it's not gonna happen," Staples says as his softball-sized fist thumps his scarred desktop for emphasis.

"I tell kids all the time that I've never met a retired gang member," Staples sums up. "They're all in prison or the cemetery."

That's a message your kids may need to hear.

Further Reading

Baker, Falcon. *Saving Our Kids from Delinquency, Drugs, and Despair.* New York: HarperCollins, 1991.

Prothrow-Stith, Deborah. *Deadly Consequences: How Violence Is Destroying Our Teenage Population.* New York: HarperCollins, 1991.

Notes

1. Deborah Prothrow-Stith, *Deadly Consequences: How Violence Is Destroying Our Teenage Population,* (New York: HarperCollins, 1991): 96–97.
2. Ibid, 108.
3. Steven Nagler, reported in "On the Streets, They Sell Ounces of Prevention," *Newsweek* (August 2, 1993): 47.

9

Guard Against Depression and Suicide

Derril was such a bright kid. Very smart. He had instant recall—if he read something once, he remembered it. And talented? He played the cello and piano and was good at sports. A kid with everything going for him.

Yet in the fall of his senior year, just before his 18th birthday, Derril asked to borrow the car for a school field trip. He took his mother to work, kissed her goodbye, returned home, plugged all the gaps in the garage with rags, swallowed a handful of pills, and ran the family car until he was dead.

"He just gave up the ship," says his father, David. "He didn't think life was worth living anymore."

Looking back, there were clues, his father says. They just didn't recognize them at the time.

Derril had been a happy, outgoing child. Gradually he changed. He became more and more stubborn. "He didn't like to be told what to do," says his father. He experimented, as do so many high school kids, with alcohol and drugs, although there were none in his blood the day he died. He had wild mood swings, avoided making any plans for the future, read demonic literature, sometimes sneaked out at night, and threatened to run away.

But, his father says, Derril had seemed happier the last few weeks before his death. He had gone for counseling. His grades were better. He was more cooperative at home. He seemed to have turned the corner.

A few days before he died, Derril gave away some of his prized possessions. His two pets—a gerbil and a tarantula—were found dead in their cages. Still no one realized what he was going to do.

It's a tragic story, this waste of a bright young man. But not an unusual one. Every year about 100,000 young people under the age of 24 attempt suicide. Five thousand succeed. That rate is triple what it was 30 years ago.[1] Between 1980 and 1992, the suicide rate rose 28 percent among youth ages 15 to 19 and 120 percent among kids ages 10 to 14 according to the Centers for Disease Control and Prevention.[2]

Recently an epidemiologist at the University of South Carolina did a survey of nearly 4,000 high school students. Eleven percent said they had had serious suicidal thoughts. Six percent had made a plan to kill themselves, and 7.5 percent had actually made an attempt.[3] More females attempt suicide but more males succeed, probably because they use more violent methods.

There are a lot of myths about suicide.

- **Those who talk about it don't do it.** That's probably the most common myth and the most destructive. People who talk about suicide *do* do it. Sure, kids tend to be dramatic, "I'll kill myself if he doesn't call tonight!" But that's not the kind of talk we mean. Comments like "I wish I weren't here anymore," "You'll be sorry when I'm gone," or "What's the use?" are clues that should not be ignored.

- **Kids just need to look at the bright side and they'll feel better.** Teens are too inexperienced at life to know that things change, that today's crisis may be forgotten tomorrow. To them, today's crisis is very real and very painful. Pointing out all the good things in their lives may just make them feel guilty.
- **Talk about suicide, or trying it, is just a way to get attention.** Everyone wants attention, but feeling so hopeless that suicide seems the only answer is not just a craving to be noticed—it's far more serious.
- **The crisis is over when the person seems to feel better.** Not necessarily. A more cheerful outlook may mean that he or she has made a decision and has the energy to do it.
- **Talking about suicide will just put the idea into the person's head.** Nonsense. If a teen is feeling desperate, asking if he is thinking about suicide won't put anything into his head that isn't already there. Having the feeling confronted may be a real relief.
- **People who commit suicide are mentally ill.** Some are. People diagnosed with schizophrenia have a high rate of suicide. So do those with clinical depression caused by a chemical imbalance in the brain. But some who commit suicide aren't mentally ill. Some are just kids so overwhelmed with stress and pain they don't know how to cope.

- **It must be the parents' fault if their child tries suicide.** Parents often feel enormous guilt and shame if their child attempts suicide. Their first question might be "Where did we go wrong?" But most parents do the best job they can with the information and skills they have. Almost no parent wants to hurt their child. Parents are not responsible for all the choices kids make.[4]

What drives a teenager to make the terrible choice to end his or her life? Debra Reid, a clinical social worker whose private practice has included extensive work with adolescents, says many times a teenager who makes an attempt doesn't really intend to die. "They intend to stop the pain," she says. "They want that pain that they feel so eaten by to stop, and they don't know how to do that."

Often the young person is depressed. "Not everybody who is depressed is suicidal, but almost everybody who is suicidal is depressed," Reid says. She points out that *depressed* can mean a painfully sad emotional state or it can mean a clinical depression caused by a chemical imbalance in the brain. It's sometimes hard to know which you are dealing with. It may take assessment by a mental health professional to find out.

There are, Reid says, some factors which put a child at higher risk for suicide:

- **A prior attempt.**
- **A family member or close friend who has committed suicide.**
- **A "family lifestyle" of depression.** Some families

have a history of depression, which may be genetic or behavioral.

- **Drug and alcohol use.** Both can make a chemical imbalance worse. Substance abuse also can intensify aggressive feelings, which makes kids more vulnerable to anger and poor decision-making.
- **Unsettled sexual identity.** A teen might be feeling unattractive, uncomfortable about the opposite sex, fearful of being homosexual, or afraid of sexual feelings.
- **A dramatic change in family life,** especially divorce or remarriage.
- **A great deal of stress and limited coping skills.** The person might be experiencing academic pressures, the breakup of a romance, the failure to make a team, or rejection by peers.
- **A pattern of violent or aggressive behavior.** The individual might also engage in dangerous activities or have had brushes with the law. In the previously cited University of South Carolina study, teens who exhibited the most aggressive behavior had the highest chance of thinking about, planning, or attempting suicide.[5]
- **In direct contrast to the above factor, persons at risk may exhibit a pattern of shyness and isolation.**
- **Physical or sexual abuse** by a family member, trusted friend, or acquaintance, especially for girls.
- **Rigid, black-and-white thinking patterns.**

- **Clinical depression or mental illness.**

Signs to Watch For

The signs that a teen is depressed and those that indicate thoughts of suicide often overlap, which is not surprising since depression is often a component of suicide. Signs of depression include:

- Loss of interest in usual activities.
- Change in appetite or a weight gain or loss.
- Change in sleep patterns, either too little or too much, especially insomnia at night and sleeping during the day.
- Loss of energy, listlessness.
- Blaming oneself for everything that goes wrong, whether or not that's reasonable.
- Negative self-image, expression of self-contempt.
- Air of sadness, hopelessness, or worry.
- Inability to concentrate or pay attention.
- Aggressive behavior or conversely, withdrawal.
- Agitation, restlessness.
- Increased physical aches and pains.
- Decline in schoolwork.
- Morbid thoughts.[6]

Signs of suicidal tendencies in a child include all of the above, Reid says, plus:

- Any attempt at bodily harm, no matter how minor.
- Verbal threats such as "I can't take it anymore" or

"You'd be better off without me."

- Preoccupation with death. Talking, writing, drawing pictures, or watching movies about death. An unhealthy occupation with symbols or objects representing death. Reading books by authors who have committed suicide.
- Withdrawal from family, friends, and normal activities.
- Violent, rebellious behavior such as playing with weapons, breaking the law, running away, or explosive outbursts.
- Using drugs and alcohol.
- Giving away valued possessions such as clothing or favorite CDs. Making arrangements for pets.
- An unexplained "high" or cheerful mood after a period of depression. This may be a signal that the person has decided on suicide and made a plan.
- The suicide of a friend or admired celebrity.
- Skipping school. Most kids are absent from school the day before their attempt.

The actual attempt is often precipitated by a painful or humiliating event, such as the breakup of a romance, an encounter with the law, or rejection by a team or college.

Preventing Suicide

While it's true that it can be very difficult to stop someone who is truly bent on self-destruction, there are things parents can do early on to tip the odds toward keeping a troubled young person alive and helping him or her work toward a happier life.

First, there are some things you can do to foster a general atmosphere in your home to prevent a child from becoming depressed and suicidal, says Reid.

- **Tell your kids you love them.** "Sometimes it's hard to love a teenager unconditionally!" Reid laughs. "But you must, and more than that, you must tell them you do. Kids don't get that message by osmosis. They have to hear it."

- **Tell them that God loves them.** "Kids who see God as a punishing authority are more at risk because they may see no way out of their problems," Reid says. Read Jeremiah 29:11 with your children: " 'I know the plans I have for you,' declares the Lord, 'plans to prosper you and not to harm you, plans to give you hope and a future.' " God has claimed your children as His own in Baptism. Their future is well-planned—a home in heaven, thanks to the redeeming work of our Lord Jesus Christ. As you face decisions, ask your children to join you in discussion and prayer. Tell them often that no struggle is too hopeless or no despair too deep that Jesus cannot help them through it.

- **Maintain open communication in your home.** That advice seems to turn up in every chapter, which shows how vital it is. Communication is the foundation for good parenting. Let your kids know they can talk to you about anything. And when they do, don't jump all over them if they say something you find difficult to handle.

- **If you are struggling with your own problems, get help.** If parents are depressed, chances are their kids will be too. Don't let your mood infect your children.

- **Be sure you have dealt with unresolved conflicts in your own background.** Some parents see their teenagers dealing with the same problems they never resolved. Their own pain is so great that they try to deny their children's problems.

If you pick up some clues that suggest your teen is depressed or suicidal, you need to act, and you need to do it without delay. Here are some suggestions from Reid and other experts.

- **Don't panic.** But at the same time, trust your judgment. If you think something is going on, go with it.

- **Never ignore a threat or a verbal warning,** even if you think your child is not serious.

- **Be extra vigilant** if your teen experiences a serious loss, especially if it's the suicide of a friend, acquaintance, or even an admired rock star.

- **Demonstrate your support.** Show that you are concerned and that you don't want your child to do anything harmful. Ask specific questions: "Are you thinking about suicide?" "Have you decided how you would do it?" "Have you done anything about it?" You have to show, Reid says, that you are not afraid of what your child is thinking, which

may in turn reduce the teen's level of fear.
- **Tell your child that he or she doesn't have to be miserable,** that unhappiness is not normal, that there are ways to make life better. Kids sometimes think that everyone feels depressed.
- **Remove all potentially dangerous items from your home,** including weapons, drugs, alcohol, and the car keys. Kids can be impulsive.
- **Don't leave your child alone.**
- **Get professional help** *immediately.* You can't deal with this alone. Don't give in to feelings of secrecy and shame. Depression is an illness, a temporary illness, and nothing to be ashamed of.

You can find help in several ways. If the emergency is acute (your child has done something harmful or is on the verge of doing so), take him or her to an emergency room, preferably at a hospital with an adolescent psychiatric unit. Even if it's not an acute emergency, don't let too much time go by.

To find a mental health professional, consult a hospital, pediatrician, your child's school, a friend who has had counseling, or your pastor. Not all pastors have the experience to handle a suicidal person, but they will probably know someone who does. A Christian counselor who can assure your child of God's grace and forgiveness is best, but if you can't find one, the basics of saving a life can still be accomplished.

There are a few things you should *not* do, Reid says.

- **Don't ever promise that you won't tell anyone, especially the other parent.** "It's too important that the teen get help—losing temporary trust is better than losing a life," Reid says. When she works with troubled kids, she tells them up front that she will keep confidential anything but threats to harm themselves or someone else.

- **Don't appear shocked or panicked.** It's hard to remain calm, but your child needs your calming influence.

- **Don't be judgmental.** "This is not the time to quote Scripture about the morals of suicide," Reid says. "That will only increase any sense of guilt and shame." Instead, talk about God's love. Even better, model it. Be the most loving, supportive, nonjudging parent you can be.

If someone you love is suicidal, it's important that you know what the church says about suicide. Rev. Harold Senkbeil, who has dealt with several suicide cases, says he always thinks of Martin Luther's comment. "Luther once said that suicide is like getting jumped in an alley," Senkbeil says. "That means it isn't always a deliberate act. It's often simply being overpowered by things, internal or external. We cannot assume that God is going to automatically condemn everybody who commits suicide. The church has a message of both Law and Gospel, so in the face of suicide, we proclaim both."

Derril, the young man at the beginning of this chapter, seems like a classic case of teen suicide. He exhibited so many of the characteristics and warning signals. His parents did try to get him help. They went for family and individual counseling. But in his case, it was not successful.

That doesn't mean there's no hope for depressed kids. On the contrary, says Reid, "There absolutely *is* hope." Depression can be helped with therapy. And medication should be considered. It can be very helpful for some teens.

"The sooner you deal with depression, the better," Reid points out. "The deeper you get into the hole, the harder it can be to climb out. Sometimes adults have been depressed for years, but the good news about adolescent depression is that you're at the top of the hole. You haven't gone down too far."

The biggest barrier to getting help, she emphasizes, is fear. "Some people are so paralyzed by fear, they do nothing. They think if they don't talk about it, it will go away," Reid explains. But it won't. Confronting the depression and getting help is the only answer.

Further Reading

Oster, Gerald, and Sarah Montgomery. *Helping Your Depressed Teenager.* John Wiley and Sons, 1995.

Shamoo, Tonia K., and Philip G. Patros. *I Want to Kill Myself: A Parent's Guide to Understanding Depression and Suicide in Children.* New York: Free Press, 1990.

Notes

1. Elizabeth Royte, "They Seemed so Normal," *Health* (November/December, 1994): 77.
2. United States Centers for Disease Control and Prevention, as

quoted in the *Washington Post*, (May 1995).
3. B. Bower, "Suicide Signs Loom in Pair of Surveys," *Science News* (February 13, 1993): 101.
4. Tonia K. Shamoo, and Philip G. Patros, *I Want to Kill Myself: A Parent's Guide to Understanding Depression and Suicide in Children*, (New York: Free Press, 1990): 29.
5. Bower, 52.
6. Ibid, 102.

10
Fight Eating Disorders

To look at Bobbi you'd never guess that two years ago the bones of her 5' 7" body were wrapped in just a few inches of flesh. At 95 pounds there was barely enough meat to pad her behind when she sat. Every knob on every bone was visible through her papery skin. Victim of a concentration camp? Locked in a closet and starved? No. Bobbi did it to herself.

Anorexia nervosa (often abbreviated in the press as anorexia) and its cousin bulimia are, some experts say, reaching epidemic proportions among America's young women—and to a lesser extent, young men.

Anorexia isn't a new disease. It was written about in the psychiatric literature of the 1800s where it was referred to as a "strange wasting disease of women." In the late 1960s and early '70s, it began to receive recognition as a diagnosable disorder. Effective treatments were developed during the late 1970s and have continued to improve, but anorexia is still largely underdiagnosed.

Bobbi fought her battle with anorexia in college, as do so many young people, but she's convinced it started much earlier. "I've had it for a long time," she says. "I think it starts very young. For me it started in grade school with a really bad body image. By high school my best friend would get angry at me anytime we were going anywhere because I'd keep asking, 'Do I *really* look okay?' It just meant so much to me."

Bobbi, with her long blonde hair and liquid, dark eyes, had no reason to doubt how attractive she really was. Yet she did. "I remember sitting there hating my body, wishing I could just chop it off," she says with a shudder of her still slim shoulders.

That, says Dr. Laura Lees, director of an eating disorders clinic at a psychiatric hospital, is typical of a young girl starting the battle with anorexia.

The term *anorexia*, Dr. Lees points out, simply means weight loss. *Anorexia nervosa* is a more specific term that means a deliberate starving of the self. Anorexics cannot understand that they are too thin. They stubbornly insist that they need to shed more pounds from their already bony frames. About 90 percent of anorexics are female. About one in 200 women will have the disorder. The majority are Caucasian, from ages 12 to 25, but the disease can and does occur in all ages, races, sexes, and social and economic classes.

In a related eating disorder, bulimia, the patient typically binges on huge amounts of food and then purges the body of what was eaten. A bulimic throws up, uses laxatives, starves herself, or overexercises (especially common in males) to compensate for the overeating. Some experts fear that as many as 25 percent of college-aged women engage in binging and purging.

Society Says, "Be Thin"

"There's such a lot of pressure on girls and women

to be thin, to look like models," Dr. Lees says. "When adolescent girls look at a magazine, they don't realize that most of those models are seriously underweight."

Dr. Lees doesn't think our society realizes what effect those messages have on young children. "We're finding now that 50 to 60 percent of 10-year-old girls are on a diet," she says. "We hear 5- and 6-year-old girls talking about how fat they are."

Those children's mothers grew up in the era of Twiggy not the more curvaceous Marilyn Monroe. They themselves are very weight and diet conscious. "Children are going to pick that up," Dr. Lees says.

Anorexia and bulimia often develop when people try to achieve and maintain a body size and shape that's in conflict with their biology, she explains. Of course, being overweight isn't good either because carrying too many pounds increases the risk of heart disease and diabetes. But expecting a body that isn't genetically predisposed to slimness to be the size and shape of a pencil can be just as harmful as obesity.

Family Troubles

A second major cause of anorexia, according to Dr. Lees, is what's going on in the family. "In most anorexics you see very controlling parents, parents who don't want children to have, or to talk about, feelings" she says. "They want everything to look fine to the outside world—we are the perfect family."

That syndrome sometimes exists in Christian families when parents feel their image as the perfect family must be maintained at all costs. "These parents are God-fearing people and they want to look perfect in their church community," Dr. Lees explains. "But when you step away from the church scene and into their homes, there can be extreme dysfunction."

Kids cooperate with this scenario. They learn to put up a front. "When you see a family that seems perfect, that has no problems or conflict, that's a red flag," Dr. Lees says. "No family is without problems. Some conflict is normal."

Anorexic families often don't allow much room for individuality, she says. Children are required to be miniature adults. They aren't allowed to make any messes. They aren't allowed to have opinions that differ from those of their parents. And they certainly aren't allowed to express any anger. Parents in these families may be overly involved in their children's lives, allowing them no physical or emotional privacy. Parents may be overprotective and not allow the child to make—and learn from—mistakes. Parents with poor self-esteem themselves may live through their children's achievements, placing unrealistic expectations on them.

Bobbi sees a lot of her family in that description. Her successful businessman father wasn't around much. While her mother did have some personal identity because of her secretarial job at a real estate office, she was very concerned about how the family appeared to members of their church. "I couldn't do things like have boys over because of what people would think," Bobbi recalls. "My mother was so obsessed with appearances. We had to have the perfect house. She cleaned before the cleaning service came—not making your bed was a sin."

When puberty hit, conflict escalated. "I was always

mad at my parents," Bobbi says. "They did things I didn't think were fair. I never spoke nicely to them, especially to my mom. I did have a bad mouth."

Bobbi's older brother seemed perfect to her. He was good-looking, athletic, and got good grades—everything she wanted for herself. "He had the best friends," she recalls. "I had my own friends, but I wanted his. I wanted to be him. I just didn't think my needs were being met. I didn't think I was being seen. Maybe that's why I wanted to disappear."

A family style that can also cause problems, Dr. Lees says, is the opposite of the controlling family—the chaotic one where there are no boundaries, no rules, and no consistency. "The child almost becomes the parent in order to establish some kind of order," she says. Often in these families, the parents abuse drugs or alcohol, staying "high," and no one is available to take care of the children.

Other causes of anorexia can include physiological and emotional problems. Research suggests that some eating disorders, although not all, have a genetic component. Some bulimics in particular respond to antidepressant medications, which indicates a possible brain chemical factor connected with the disease. More research needs to be done in this area.

Many anorexics have emotional problems, but which comes first—the problem or the anorexia—can be hard to determine. Anorexics may feel worthless and inadequate. They may be such perfectionists that they allow themselves no mistakes. They often don't have strong, stable identities and may fear losing the approval of others if they don't measure up to some idealistic standard. They sometimes want to be independent but are afraid of independence, so they may retreat into the safety of comfortable routines. A significant number are victims of rape or incest.[1]

Once started on the cycle of starvation, the physical consequences come quickly and can be severe.

- Wasted muscles. The heart is also a muscle, and it can shrink, resulting in a heart attack from sudden exertion. It also can lose its normal rhythm and cause sudden death.
- Dry, thin skin; brittle, peeling nails; hair loss; and low body temperature.
- Fragile, easily broken bones.
- Slowdown of the digestive organs and abdominal bloating. Excessive laxative use can cause bowel function to stop.
- Damage to the esophagus, teeth, and gums from constant vomiting.

Bobbi's problems escalated once she left home for college. She chose a tough, Ivy League school to prove something to her family and friends. "I went to the best college I could get into, but I was scared," she says. "I thought I had to be smart. My parents and friends all thought I was smart, but I didn't think so."

While she loved college, the pressure made her "eat her way through." The "freshman 15" turned into 30. She failed one class and that drove her to eat more. She couldn't let anyone know she was scared. "I was a '90s woman. I could do it alone!"

During her sophomore year, Bobbi and a group of friends decided to diet together. As she watched the weight melt from her best friends, she felt driven to do even better. Then came the discovery that almost proved fatal. "I found that all I had to do to lose weight was to stop eating."

That summer Bobbi lived on an occasional lettuce sandwich and the pounds dropped. Cheekbones jutted beneath ever-larger eyes. She looked dramatic but on the edge of gaunt. She learned to make herself throw up, which meant she could eat just enough so her parents wouldn't notice anything was wrong.

Bobbi returned to school in the fall painfully thin. Her thoughts seemed scattered. She was always cold and her hair was falling out. Paradoxically, she did better than ever on her schoolwork. Her friends, who had all reached their goal weights, watched in horror as Bobbi's bones poked through her pale skin.

Bobbi's life spun out of control. Admission to a psychiatric hospital only made her more rebellious and determined not to eat. Fearing she would go into cardiac arrest, the doctors put a feeding tube down her throat. "It hurt so much I promised to eat if they took it out," she says. But once it came out, she ate only enough to keep her nurses happy and threw up behind their backs. "That hospital didn't help me, but I wasn't ready to be helped," she recalls.

Treatment Can Be Effective

Once the person is ready to confront the reality of her illness, says Dr. Lees, there are effective treatments. "But it's absolutely critical that she see someone who specializes in treating eating disorders, who understands the physical, emotional, and psychological consequences because they have to be treated as a whole," Dr. Lees explains.

The first step in treatment is renourishment. Because starvation affects the brain, therapy can't be effective until the brain is working properly again. If the anorexic is in danger of dying, and many are, hospitalization for tube feeding may be necessary.

Treatment, which can include individual therapy, group therapy, family therapy, and nutritional counseling, often must be long-term. The disease can become chronic. The rate of relapse is very high. "But people can and do recover," Dr. Lees says. "They learn to recognize and deal with feelings and how to cope with them without starvation."

Bobbi is a good example. Discharged from the first hospital, she went home, frantic at having lost a semester of school. She insisted on returning to school in January. Her parents agreed only if she would see a therapist. "It was a God-directed thing that I found the right one," Bobbi says now.

The new therapist wasn't fooled. She knew Bobbi was lying to everyone about how much she was eating. She knew Bobbi couldn't stop her harmful behavior by herself. The therapist also knew of a hospital that specialized in eating disorders. After one particularly devastating binge and purge, Bobbi finally admitted she needed help and agreed to go. "It was almost a relief," she recalls. "I couldn't do it anymore. I needed someone to take care of me."

A month in the second hospital, followed by a year

of outpatient group therapy, finally turned Bobbi's life around. Today, still slim but not emaciated, she's going to school part-time while working and trying to build a life for herself.

"It's hard. Recovery is very hard," Bobbi says. "It's much harder than being sick. It's hard every day because you are living a real life and dealing with emotions and consequences. Recovery is a process. I will never not be an anorexic; I will always be a recovering anorexic."

Prevention

First, you as a parent need to be aware of the behavior that can indicate your child is in trouble. The earlier the problem is found, the easier it is to deal with. Not every anorexic will be all the following things, but a developing pattern is cause for concern.

- **Excessive weight loss.**
- **Stubborn refusal to eat** even when hungry, irritable or lightheaded from lack of food.
- **Compulsive exercise,** usually a solitary activity such as running rather than a team sport.
- **Inaccurate body image.** Saying "I'm so fat" when the child is obviously not overweight. Constant weighing, often several times a day.
- **Development of strange rituals around food** such as cooking and serving it a certain way or hiding it. Preoccupation with shopping for food, storing it, and counting every calorie. Preparing elaborate meals for others but not eating.

- **Perfectionism in other aspects of life,** including appearance, grades, relationships, sports, neatness, and organization. Black-and-white thinking—everything is bad or good, no shades of gray.
- **Change in wardrobe.** Dressing in layers to hide thinness. Being constantly cold. Heavy sweaters in summer weather.
- **Spending a lot of time in the bathroom,** especially after meals. Parents may hear sounds of vomiting, vigorously denied by the child.[2]

Far better than treatment is prevention. There are things you as a Christian parent can do so your child doesn't feel the need to starve herself to make a statement. The following suggestions come from Dr. Lees and Bobbi.

- **Look at your parenting style.** Are you overly controlling? Give your child space. Let her develop into an individual. This is not to say you shouldn't have high standards or guide your child—remember that a chaotic home life is also destructive. But don't try to run every aspect of your child's life.
- **Christian children can be naughty too.** Don't expect your child to be perfect in everything, all the time. Model God's forgiveness and acceptance for your child. Remind your child that Jesus died for us while we were still sinners. God loves and accepts us, not on our merit but through the sacrifice of His Son.
- **Have interests of your own.** Develop your own ways to build your self-esteem so you don't live

through your child's accomplishments or place unrelenting pressure on her. Remember that true self-esteem stems from what Christ did for us on the cross. Reminding yourself and your child that you are God's precious children will help you value yourselves.

- **Allow your children to express feelings.** Teach them to deal with anger in constructive ways instead of saying, "Don't feel that way."
- **Don't make food an issue in your home.** If you must diet, don't dwell on it or make it the central topic of conversation. Avoid "good food/bad food" labels.
- **Don't make eating or not eating a power struggle.** You'll lose.
- **Don't call your child fat or tease her about her weight.** An overweight child needs healthier eating patterns and more exercise, not shame, blame, and a strict diet.
- **Feed your child emotionally.** "I wish my parents had let me know that I was okay," Bobbi says.
- **Make sure your child knows that God created her body and that it is good.** Try to instill a feeling that bodies come in various sizes and shapes, and they're all God's creation.
- **Communicate, communicate, communicate.** Through words and touch, let your child feel the warmth of your love every day. No emotional putdowns.
- **Listen, listen, listen.** When your child tells you something, don't just jump in with a solution. Lis-

ten to the feelings behind the statements.

If you suspect your child is struggling with anorexia, get professional help. This is not something you as a parent can deal with alone. Anorexia puts enormous strains on families. You may benefit from some counseling too.

While Bobbi's experience was wrenching for her and her family, some good things did come out of it. She and her parents are on better terms now. They've worked through some of their areas of conflict. And she says, her faith is even stronger and more personal now. "I'm so grateful for my Christian background," she says. "I didn't grow up with a 'God-is-harsh' picture. I have a loving faith and that has grown. I'm more open now, open to learn about who I am and what God is to me."

Notes

1. ANRED (Anorexia Nervosa and Related Eating Disorders), Eugene, Oregon, "Eating Disorders Information Packet."
2. Ibid.

For further information on anorexia nervosa and other eating disorders, contact ANRED, P.O. Box 5102, Eugene, OR 97405; (503) 344-1144. Or contact the National Association of Anorexia Nervosa and Associated Disorders, Inc., Box 271, Highland Park, IL 60035; (312) 831-3448.

11

Arm Your Kids to Battle Satanism

Just north of the city of Milwaukee, Wisconsin, where the Lake Michigan shoreline curves in a gentle S, lies a stretch of secluded beach. Rough and natural, there's no city-maintained, well-groomed public swimming area here. Instead waves crash onto rock-littered sand. Sand pipers skitter and clumps of storm-tossed seaweed dry in the sun. The beach is backed by a tumble of rocks and thick woods. Formidable bluffs rise high, shielding the area from the curious gaze of passers-by.

At the base of the bluffs, tucked back against the woods, is a strange formation built from beach rocks. Shaped like a giant numeral 6, it curves with the shoreline. Inside the loop of the 6 are smaller piles of rocks, next to it, a small rock tower.

A place to roast hot dogs and marshmallows? Probably not. According to Rev. David Brown of Logos Communication Consortium Inc., a group involved in research into the occult, the formation has the earmarks of a Satanic altar, including the remains of animal sacrifices.

"Our society is being saturated with the occult," Rev. Brown says. "People are trying to get wisdom and power, not through prayer and Bible study, but through sorcery, magic, and Satanism. Many, many kids are dabbling in occult practices."

Matthew, who wants to keep his identity secret, knows that firsthand. Sucked deep into Satanism during high school, and with it drug and alcohol abuse, he came close to losing his life several times. Now free from the bonds of Satan, he doesn't like remembering those lost years of his life, but says he needs to share his story to warn parents of the danger to their kids.

Matthew's father, a minister, died when Matthew was only 9 years old. "I felt so lonely," he says. "I really loved my dad, and I thought it was God's fault for taking him away from us. I really needed a male in my life, but I didn't have one."

Matthew started high school at a religious boarding school but felt lost there, alone and without friends. He spent hours in the library where he discovered books on the occult. After a few months he made friends with some town kids who weren't students at his school. They introduced him to drugs and alcohol. Expelled from the boarding school, Matthew returned home and quickly found a best friend, Karl, a young man whose stepfather seriously abused him. Together the two boys explored their mutual interest in the occult. One night, working with materials they found around the house, they made their own Ouija board. It quickly took over their lives.

Believing they were communicating with a demon, Karl asked the board to take revenge on his stepfather. The board spelled out a date and time a few weeks in the future. On that day, at that time, a strange cat wandered into the house and attacked Karl's stepfather, slashing his face badly enough to require a trip to the hospital.

"Whether that was just coincidence or was caused by a spirit, it really hooked us," Matthew says. The two boys went deeper into the occult and got some friends involved. They performed Satanic rituals, sacrificed animals, and did other things he doesn't want to talk about. "The more we got into it, the more we felt we were our own little gods and we could do anything we wanted," he says.

Matthew's story isn't unusual, says Jack Roper of Christian Apologetics Research and Information Society (CARIS), another group that researches the occult. Roper, who acts as a consultant to police departments around the country that are dealing with ritual crimes, sees ever-increasing evidence of kids involved in Satanism.

Roper points out that, while society as a whole denies the existence of Satan, the Bible very clearly tells us there is another dimension of reality that we cannot see. The Bible very clearly warns us about its dangers. "I know this stuff is real," Roper states. "I can go into any county in the United States and find the occult and Satanism."

What Is Satanism?

Imagine a world where everything is upside-down. Good is evil and evil is good. Satan is loved and worshiped; God is hated and reviled. Satanism is the perversion of Christianity. Even its symbol is an upside-down cross.

When you worship Satan, there are no laws, no rules. The Ten Commandments don't apply. Anton LaVey, founder of the Church of Satan, once said that instead of commanding its followers to repress their sinful urges as Christianity does, Satanism invites them to indulge every evil wish: sexual lust, the drive for power, revenge, and the desire for material possessions. In return for worship and loyalty, Satanism promises easy answers to complex problems, control, power, indulgence, acceptance, and fun. That's what makes Satanism so powerfully appealing to kids.

And Satanism's being sold to kids every day in very subtle ways through the mass media. Television programs—even cartoons—and movies are filled with occult themes. People get power, gain wisdom, or receive possessions through magic spells or communications with spirits or the dead. Adults see most of these films and TV programs as simple entertainment. Who wouldn't experience a warm glow watching the loving communication between an attractive young woman and her dead lover in "Ghost"? But kids may not realize movies or TV programs are only pretend. They can be subtly influenced. As Roper says, doors to the occult can be cracked open.

What Kinds of Kids Get into the Occult?

Can we predict which kids are at risk to become obsessed with the occult? To a degree but not entirely, according to Roper. "Often the kids who get into Satanism are from dysfunctional families," he says.

"While that is not always true, often they are abused or there is drug or alcohol abuse in the family."

Kids are usually lured into a fascination with the occult through peer pressure. During the teen years especially, acceptance by the peer group is all important. "There are a lot of lonely kids out there," Roper says, "Kids looking to be recognized, wanting to be part of the clique. To be part of the group, you have to go along with the group, and if it's into the occult, the kid may go along."

The usual first step, Roper says, is for the teen to have to prove himself. Usually that's done through vandalism, drinking, taking drugs, or participating in a Satanic ritual. There's a pattern of progression in which the rituals escalate in depravity. "Drugs and Satanism are almost always linked," Roper says. "And perverted sex is often part of the rituals."

Then the whole thing may become a power trip, Roper says. As the person feels more and more powerful, he or she may experiment with ever deeper aspects of the occult, including animal sacrifice, blood drinking, black magic, and demonology. Criminal activities may escalate to the point where even if the person wants to leave the group, usually called a coven, he or she may be threatened or blackmailed.

What Can Parents Do?

As dark and frightening as the world of the occult is, Christian parents need to remember that we have an even greater power on our side. The forces of darkness are no match for the power of God. God defeated Satan for all time when He sent His Son to the cross for our sin and raised Him to life again. Your child promised to fight Satan at his or her Baptism. That baptismal regeneration as God's forgiven child will help him or her deal with the trappings of the occult.

There are things you as a parent can do, first to prevent your child from ever becoming involved with the occult and secondly to help if you find your child is involved in Satanism. Let's start with prevention.

- **The atmosphere in your home.** "You must raise your child in a moral environment," says Roper. "If a child lives in a perverted environment, he will follow perverted friends." That means making your moral standards very clear and making your faith a living part of family life, not just a ritual you observe on Sunday.

- **Communication.** Most parents don't understand the occult subculture, Roper says. They don't recognize the symbols or understand the terminology. You need to do some background reading so you have a working knowledge of the topic. Then discuss it with your child. A movie or TV show about communicating with the dead or Satan worship can provide an opening. Even something as innocent as Disney's "Beauty and the Beast" can spark a discussion of magic spells and what's real and what's fantasy.

- **Teaching discernment.** Teach your children that there are two sources of wisdom, says Rev. Brown. "There is wisdom from above and wisdom from beneath. Teach them that the occult is wisdom from beneath, and it will take them where they don't want to go: to the worship of false gods, sexual immorality, drug use, and even to death."

- **Parental control.** Rev. Brown feels you should forbid occult materials—movies, comic books, magazines, games such as the Ouija board—from even coming into your house. But, he cautions, don't say no to your children without giving them a reason. Sit down with them and watch the video, look at the comic book, and point out what is wrong. Discuss it, Rev. Brown says, then turn it off or close the cover. You don't have to absorb the whole thing to know it's bad. You want your children to learn discernment. You can't be with them 24 hours a day. They have to learn what is evil and turn from it themselves.
- **Offer alternatives.** If you forbid the Ouija board, get your children a wholesome board game. If you return an occult film, rent them a wholesome one.

How can you know if your child is experimenting with the occult? Here are some signs to look for.

- Sudden hatred of family and the family religion.
- Change in friends. The new ones may look strange and threatening. A formerly open child may become secretive, not bringing friends home because he or she doesn't want you to see them.
- A drop in grades and loss of interest in former school activities such as sports or music.
- Involvement with drugs or alcohol.
- Marks on the body, including cuts and scars in

symbolic patterns. Fingernails painted black.
- Different style of dress that features lots of black. Jewelry with occult symbols.
- Occult symbols in drawings or on schoolbooks. The child may have a notebook or diary, often called the *Book of Shadows,* written in a strange alphabet or filled with occult symbols.
- A new interior decoration scheme in his or her room that often features black walls, heavy metal posters, and occult symbols.
- Presence of knives, black candles, and the smell of incense.
- Preoccupation with heavy metal rock music performed by groups with Satanic symbols on their album covers and occult references in the lyrics.

Of course, the presence of one or just a few of these clues doesn't mean your child is into Satanism. But if there are several, it should be a warning.

"Don't go bonkers," says Rev. Brown. "But talk to the child about it. Talk to your pastor. Seek the wise counsel of Godly people."

If you find in your investigation that your child is deeply involved in the occult, you have an urgent situation that you probably cannot handle yourself. You will most likely need professional help. Start with your pastor, but even he may be unable to provide counseling for this particular situation. You can turn to an organization such as CARIS for advice (the address and phone number are found at the end of this chapter). A psychologist may help, but choose a Christian who believes in the power of the occult. Some parents have been told by health professionals that fascination with the occult is just a stage, with tragic results. If drugs and alcohol are part of the picture, you may need a specialized chemical dependency program.

Don't discount the power of prayer, says Roper. "You are dealing with a supernatural dimension. You need a supernatural weapon. You need to get on your knees. Prayer is the most powerful resource you have." The sense of awe and ritual that can draw children to the occult is a positive accent of corporate worship. Talk often with your children about the faith the Holy Spirit worked in them at their Baptism, the strength He works in them as they study and hear God's Word, and the forgiveness they receive through Christ's body and blood. Pray with your child, at home and in worship. God will answer—He has already won your child's victory over Satan.

Kids who are coming out of the occult subculture will need a lot of support and follow-up. Many of them have been harassed by people still in the group. It's important to get them into healthy activities at home, school, and church to fill the void and to find a person, perhaps a youth minister or teacher, who can serve as a role model and someone to talk to.

Matthew needed a great deal of help coming out of his experience with the occult. It started with a drug rehab program. After three months in the hospital, he was convinced that if he went back to alcohol and drugs he would die. "But I was scared to die," he says, "because I knew I would go to hell because I'd rebelled against God."

On his return home he sank into depression. "I thought God could never forgive me for the things I'd done," Matthew says. "I'd always had this chemical jacket around me to shield me from the world. That was gone, but the world was still there."

Karl had moved away, but the kids Matthew drank and did drugs with were still there. "I couldn't cope with it. I felt betrayed by everything, even the demons I had served," Matthew says.

He refused to go to school and spent most days in bed. Then one afternoon while casually "channel surfing," he heard a young man talking about drugs and Satanism. "I was totally entranced by it," he recalls. "Then this TV preacher came on. I got up to turn it off, but for some reason, I didn't."

Matthew listened to the pastor talk about how God loves him and died for him. "I've heard that message all my life," Matthew says, "but I never really accepted it because I felt so guilty. But this time I felt God's love in my heart. I realized that God never left me, I left Him. And He was willing to give me another chance. I remember falling down on my knees and crying—and I hadn't cried since my dad died. I didn't say much, just 'God, forgive me.' But that's all it took."

Matthew went back to school. There a girlfriend invited him to a time-out program in which kids are released from school for an hour a week to attend religious instruction. Soon he was back in church. Matthew and his family met often with their minister and with a Christian psychologist who helped them put the family back together.

That was five years ago. Matthew has stayed clean and free from the occult ever since. The girlfriend became much more than a friend and is about to become his wife.

He's thinking about entering the ministry.

But Matthew's experiences left scars. "I call it the dumb period in my life, and I try to forget about it, as I know God has," he says. "But some things still shake me to the core, like seeing a movie about the occult. I have to leave the room."

Now Matthew speaks of Satan as the great liar. "The power I thought I saw in Satanism was a grand illusion. I was seeking acceptance, a role model, something to give meaning to my life. I thought I had found it, but look where it left me," Matthew says. "It seemed at the time that I was gaining power and respect, but in reality, I was losing it all.

"Today I have peace. I have things in Christ that are making me a better person, not destroying me," Matthew says. "There is so much rampant destruction out there, but God says His mercy is even more abundant. Even though there is total darkness, His light can shine."

A Word about Two Controversial Topics

Halloween

While most people today think of Halloween as a children's day for dressing in costumes and collecting candy, the holiday does have its roots in the occult. It is the highest holy day for Satanists and the occasion of some of their most bizarre rituals.

There are some Christians who think Halloween should have no place in the life of a believer and who do not allow their children to participate. There are others who think that as long as children know it's only pretend and they don't dress in occult costumes, it's fine. I remember my children's excitement years ago in creating their own costumes (my son's favorite was a Revolutionary War soldier) and touring the neighborhood on Sunday afternoon gathering treats.

I think you must decide for yourself whether or not to allow any Halloween celebration in your family and if you do, how it is to be done. But think about putting restrictions on what your child may choose as a costume. Occult and horror costumes may not be appropriate. On the practical side, trick-or-treating among strangers may not be safe.

If you choose not to allow your child to participate, explain carefully why. You might want to offer a special treat or outing as a substitute.

Fantasy Roleplaying Games

There are people who do research into the occult (both Jack Roper and Rev. Brown among them) who believe that fantasy roleplaying games such as *Dungeons and Dragons* open a door into the occult. They would not allow their children to play these games. There are other people who see the games as simply an exercise of the imagination, quite distinct from reality, and they treat these games as just a lot of fun.

As with Halloween, you as a parent must evaluate your own situation. You may find some of the games objectionable because of their violence or erotic imagery. Others you may find harmless. Some kids may be able to play them for a few hours like Monopoly and then walk away. Other children may become obsessed and spend so many hours playing that grades suffer and you have to place limits. If you have a highly suggestible child who takes the games so literally that he (the majority of players are boys) begins to show signs of fear or distress, obviously you must intervene. And if you sense a preoccupation with the occult, banishing the games would be wise.

If your child is interested in fantasy roleplaying games, talk to him. Find out why he enjoys them, how much time he is spending on them, whether he is clear on the line between reality and fantasy. Then make your decision. There are a couple of Christian fantasy roleplaying games available. Check your Christian bookstore.

Notes

Christian Apologetics Research and Information Service (CARIS) may be reached at P.O. Box 1659, Milwaukee, WI 53201; (414) 771-7379.